TH
GARDENING

TO ANGEL,

ENJOY!

CHARLIE

THE JOY OF GARDENING

An Inspirational Anthology

EILEEN CAMPBELL

HODDER

First published in Great Britain in 2007 by Hodder & Stoughton
An Hachette UK company

First published in paperback in 2009

2

Copyright in the arrangement © Eileen Campbell 2007
Illustration © Clare Melinsky

A CIP catalogue record for this title is available
from the British Library

ISBN 978 0 340 94368 7

Typeset in Filosofia by Avon DataSet Ltd,
Bidford-on-Avon, Warwickshire

Printed and bound in Great Britain by
Clays Ltd, St Ives plc

Hodder & Stoughton policy is to use papers that are natural, renewable
and recyclable products and made from wood grown in sustainable
forests. The logging and manufacturing processes are expected to
conform to the environmental regulations of the country of origin.

Hodder & Stoughton Ltd
338 Euston Road
London NW1 3BH
www.hodder.co.uk

To the gardeners . . . everywhere

Contents

Introduction

Gardening anthologies abound, but this one has a rather different approach to most. While it includes the writing of famous gardeners past and present, and selections from literature of all kinds, whether essays, diaries, letters, novels, plays or poems, it also includes the writings of philosophers, psychologists, mystics and spiritual teachers.

   Anthologies are always very much a personal selection, and in choosing the material for this anthology, I wanted it to appeal to all those who love gardens, whether active, hands-on gardeners, or those who simply enjoy gardens. Gardening is more than a hobby or interest – it's a way of life, which affects not only our physical health but also our emotional, psychological and spiritual well-being. I wanted to convey the joy of gardening through the seasons, and to inspire reflection on what gardening can teach us about life itself, as well as the qualities it might help develop in us – qualities like patience, optimism, trust, discipline and attention – which can ultimately help us live a fulfilled life and find happiness. Day after day we learn not only what works in the garden but also what works in our own lives too. In working with the cycles of nature, which we learn as gardeners to do, we also become more aware of that vitally important relationship between ourselves and the natural world, and are more likely to develop an ecological consciousness – of more importance today than ever before in history.

For gardeners and garden writers a diary, letters or books have been ways of sharing experiences and opinions and offering advice. While they may provide forthright views on plants and design, they often offer lyrical descriptions of plants or gardens which fire our imaginations and delight us. For novelists and playwrights gardens may be a backdrop against which a plot unfolds; for poets, plants, the seasons, or gardens can be used to convey emotion or capture poignantly some aspect of the subject or make a profound statement;

for philosophers, mystics and spiritual teachers of different traditions, East or West, plants and gardens can provide useful metaphors.

Writers have always written about gardens, whether a description of their own garden, or a garden they have seen, or even a mythical garden or an imaginary one. Their writing lives on long after the garden that inspired them has been reclaimed by nature, for gardens rarely continue as they were, unless there is an effort to conserve them. And their evocations inspire us, and make us want to create our own gardens, even if that may be just a small collection of pots or a box on a window sill.

We're fortunate that descriptions of gardens live on in literature, as they do too in buildings and pottery, in art and in music. Going back to the earliest dawn of civilisation, plants appear in decorative motifs on buildings and pottery and for personal ornamentation, long before records of garden layouts. But the wealth of literary output concerning plants and gardens is amazing, and reflects the great love of gardens and gardening through the ages.

But why is it that gardens have been such an inspiration to so many? Why too do we garden enthusiasts feel inspired at a certain stage of our lives to create our own garden? And why is it that gardens and the activity of gardening have the power to make us happy and heal our sadness?

Gardening seems to fulfil a human need to be in touch with nature. All civilisations seem to have revered nature, and the earliest rituals were linked with the earth and its fertility and the need for sun and rain. Plants and gardens were valued and the idea of a sanctuary, a place of beauty, where people can be at peace appears in all cultures. Creating and tending a garden seems to fulfil a longing for paradise on earth, as a place to which to retreat from the bustle of the world and lose oneself in contemplation. It is perhaps no coincidence that the Persian word for a garden is *'pairidaeza'*, from which the English word 'paradise' derives.

And to quote an old aphorism, 'Paradise is nearer to you than the thongs of your sandals'. All it requires is being out in the fresh air and working with the soil and plants (even if only on a balcony, or in a pocket-handkerchief of a garden by the back door). Simply sowing seed, watching life emerge, weeding, pruning, harvesting and clearing give a satisfying rhythm to life. When we're dedicated and put in the effort, we lose ourselves in the activity. We seem to transcend time itself and taste eternity. We experience joy and our souls are nourished. And as we watch the seasons turn one into another we appreciate the regenerative cycle of nature, and feel connected to something greater than ourselves.

Perhaps in the 21st century we need more than ever something to help us counter the effects of technological progress, consumerism and the cult of celebrity. We live in an era when we've lost all confidence in both politics and business and their lack of real values. Many people are unfulfilled in their lives even though they have everything they thought they wanted, while the rest of the world is caught up in poverty or war. We have somehow become divorced from the natural world and seem on a headlong course to destroy the planet one way or another. It's no wonder the 'good life' of Aristotle increasingly beckons. Not that gardening is a panacea for the problems of the world, but maybe in creating our own little bit of paradise we can as individuals make a difference. If we stay sane in an increasingly insane world, then maybe we can have an effect on others. And if we garden organically we may also be helping the environment at least a little.

For as long as I can remember I've had a passion for gardens. From early childhood, when I was eager to help my grandparents in their cottage garden; to having my very own mini-garden aged seven, where I grew both flowers and vegetables (with a great deal of help from my father); to my early twenties, when, gardenless, I endeavoured to grow tomatoes, aubergines and peppers, as well as flowers, in an assortment of pots and boxes on the window sills of a flat in the inner city. Later on, when I had my first tiny garden and greenhouse, such was my enthusiasm I grew far more in my greenhouse than I could possibly plant out in the garden. Since then I've had three gardens, where I've tried to make something of what I found – dreaming, toiling, sighing and laughing at the sheer joy of watching a garden unfold. In the process I have learned about both gardening and myself.

Gardening has for me been both a delight in good times and a consolation in times of difficulty. It has also taught me a great deal. Not only have I become familiar with plants and trees and their likes and dislikes, learned about the nature of soil and mastered the art of compost-making, raised seedlings, planted bulbs and grown vegetables – all things which any gardener learns over time – but more importantly I've learned some important life lessons from my garden, above all how to be happy living in harmony with the cycles of nature.

The Joy of Gardening is designed for garden-lovers as an anthology to inspire. Its aim is to raise the spirits merely by browsing its pages, and I hope it will leave you happier than when you first opened it. It can be turned to at any time of the year amid the gardener's never-ending round of tasks. For me it's been a privilege to work on this during the darker days of winter.

The quotations are organised by season and juxtaposed to allow the reader to reflect on the ideas. The seasonal introductions emphasise the process of birth, bloom, decay and regeneration in nature. May you enjoy endless hours of happiness in and out of the garden!

Spring

Winter gives way to spring gradually, but the signs of growth are clearly visible, and fill us with hope and optimism. As the days lengthen, sunshine and rain encourage a gentle greening of the vegetation. Arctic winds may still surprise us, frost can occasionally make a visitation and low cloud temporarily hide the sun, but those dark, cold days of winter, which seemed so endless, are finally over.

So now, effort is required to clear up after winter and re-establish some kind of order. As in life, nothing worthwhile is achieved without it. Pruning and cutting back are essential in the garden, as is the division of perennials if we want to make the best of everything. Pruning out the deadwood of our own lives, eliminating what is no longer productive, is similarly important if we are to allow new growth and opportunities to emerge.

Daily miracles seem to unfold in early spring as new life pushes through the hard surface of the earth, where all was so seemingly lifeless and dead. It's a veritable resurrection. Green shoots of lupins and delphiniums and soft green buds of camellias and tulips are full of promise. Pink and white blossom begins to cover the flowering cherry trees, while crocuses explode with their brilliant saffron and purple flowers, and the soft blue scillas and golden daffodils begin to appear.

Day by day, as the light and warmth increase and gentle rain encourages growth, the weeds too begin to appear. It's essential to get on top of them and prevent them spreading, or they will overpower and choke the plants and shrubs we are nurturing. We can never do anything but control them for a short length of time so it's a constant challenge to work with nature as best we can.

As the soil begins to warm up, it's time for sowing of seeds and planting vegetables. The soil must be our first priority, however – without proper preparation and care, nothing can come to fruition, as with any project of importance in life that we might want to undertake. If the ground was not dug and manured in the autumn, then it's time for remedial action, digging and fertilising with compost and an appropriate organic feed. Even if we did prepare the ground in the autumn, there's still the need to hoe the soil to a fine tilth. Winter may have done its work, with frost breaking up the clods of heavy soil, and with the earthworms drawing down the goodness from the surface, but the structure of the soil is vital to ensure plants get the water and nutrients they need to be productive, so the soil has to be made friable.

But it's also important to lean on the spade from time to time, and marvel at the extraordinariness of spring, epitomised by the miracle of the bulb. With its flower curled up inside when planted in the autumn, with everything it needs for its growth, it delights us as it transforms itself into the perfect spring bloom. Similarly, there is nothing more awe-inspiring than seeds – gathered in autumn, sown in spring, blossoming in summer, and dying down once fruit and seed have been produced for the following year.

What a joy to be out in the fresh air again after the cold and wet has confined us indoors – whether working in the garden or tending window boxes, or simply admiring someone else's efforts. We feel connected to nature as all around us birds twitter, gathering twigs and moss for their nests. Life in the ponds begins to stir again and we catch a glimpse of iridescence as fish swim nearer the surface, and on a warm day frogs and newts are in evidence, emerging to enjoy the spring and mate. We cannot help but feel deep respect for the life all around us, and as we work we feel that sense of co-creation, working in partnership with nature, in a world of transient beauty.

As we waken to glorious spring mornings, surrounded everywhere by soft green foliage, pendulous drifts of blossom, and the colour and scent of spring flowers, hope springs eternal. Life never fails us, but goes on and on. If that is so in the natural world, and we can experience it, season after season, year after year, why should we be any different from the rest of creation when we have run our cycle?

He who plants a garden, plants happiness.

   ᕙ Chinese proverb

. . . The lesson I have thoroughly learnt, and wish
to pass on to others is to know the enduring
happiness that the love of a garden gives . . . For
love of gardening is a seed that once sown never
dies, but always grows and grows to an enduring
and ever-increasing source of happiness.

   ᕙ *Gertrude Jekyll*, Wood and Garden, *1899*

God Almighty first planted a garden. And indeed it
is the purest of human pleasures. It is the greatest
refreshment to the spirits of man, without which
buildings and palaces are but gross handiworks.

   ᕙ *Francis Bacon*, 'Of Gardens', Essays Civil and
     Moral, *1625*

In the day that the Lord God made the earth and the heavens, and every plant of the field before it was in the earth, and every herb of the field before it grew (for the Lord God had not caused it to rain upon the earth, and there was not a man to till the ground) there went up a mist from the earth, and watered the whole face of the ground.

And the Lord God formed man of the dust of the ground and breathed into his nostrils the breath of life, and man became a living soul.

And the Lord planted a garden eastward in Eden . . . And out of the ground made the Lord God to grow every tree that is pleasant to the sight, and good for food . . . And a river went out of Eden to water the garden . . .

☙ *Genesis 2:5–10*

Go forwarde in the name of god, graffe, set, plant, and nourish up trees in every corner of your ground.

☙ *John Gerard*, Herball, *1597*

To plant trees is to give body and life to one's dreams of a better world.

❧ *Russell Page*, The Education of a Gardener, *1962*

Spring returns like clockwork, year after year, bringing with it a reminder of our true essential nature, our oneness with the planet, the stars, sun, moon, soil, rock, earth. Along with the budding leaves and flowers, something in us opens up, lets down its guard, and bursts forth. The sun stays longer and fills our minds, hearts, and bodies with more light and life . . . As I turn my attention to my garden, I am filled with gratitude for this moment in the year when all is fresh and new. It is truly like being young again, like having nothing but possibilities before me.

❧ *Veronica Ray*, Zen Gardening, *1996*

Blasted with sighs, and surrounded with teares,
Hither I come to seeke the spring,
And at mine eyes, and at my eares,
Receive such balmes, as else cure every thing . . .

☙ *John Donne*, 'Twickenham Garden', *1633*

You must stand still; and then you will see open
lips and furtive glances, tender fingers, and raised
arms, the fragility of a baby, and the rebellious
outburst of the will to live, and then you will hear
the infinite march of buds faintly roaring.

☙ *Karel Čapek*, The Gardener's Year, *1929*

Planting a garden is an act of optimism. When you
plant a seed, you put hope in the ground. Your trust
is in the future when there is no present sign that
life will come.

☙ *Marilyn Barrett*, Creating Eden, *1992*

If there is any living thing which might explain to us the mystery beyond this life, it should be seeds. We pour them curiously into the palm, dark as mystery, brown or gray as earth, bright sometimes with scarlet of those beads worked into Buddhist rosaries. We shake them there, gazing, but there is no answer to this knocking on the door. They will not tell where their life has gone, or if it is there, any more than the lips of the dead.

∽ *Donald Culross Peattie*, Flowering Earth, *1939*

The very act of planting a seed in the earth has in it to me something beautiful . . . I watch my garden beds after they are sown, and think how one of God's exquisite miracles is going on beneath the dark earth out of sight.

∽ *Celia Thaxter*, An Island Garden, *1894*

Scatter ye seeds each passing year,
Sow amid winds and storms of rain,
Hope gives the courage,
Faith casts out fear,
God will requite thee
With infinite grain.

Farmer's Almanac, 1854

It was a perfect day
For sowing; just
As sweet and dry was the ground
As tobacco-dust.

I tasted deep the hour
Between the far
Owl's chuckling first soft cry
And the first star.

A long stretched hour it was;
Nothing undone
Remained; the early seeds
All safely sown.

And now, hark at the rain,
Windless and light,
Half a kiss, half a tear,
Saying good-night.

Edward Thomas, 'Sowing', *1915*

We call upon the land which grows our food, the
nurturing soil, the fertile fields,
the abundant gardens and orchards, and we ask that
they teach us, and show us the Way . . .

Chinook blessing litany

And what is it to work with love? . . .
It is to sow seeds with tenderness and reap the
harvest with joy, even as if your beloved were to eat
the fruit . . .

Kahlil Gibran, The Prophet, *1923*

Love was the inventor, and is still the maintainer, of every noble science. It is chiefly that which hath made my flowers and trees to flourish, though planted in a barren desert, and hath brought me to the knowledge I now have in plants and planting: for indeed it is impossible for any man to have any considerable collection of noble plants to prosper, unless he love them; for neither the goodness of the soil, nor the advantages of the situation, will do it, without the master's affection; it is that which animates, and renders them strong and vigorous; without which they will languish and decay through neglect, and soon cease to do him service.

❧ *John Rea*, Flora: seu De Florum Cultura, seventeenth century

I beheld, thinking what manner of labour it might be that the servant should do. And then I understood that he should do the greatest labour and the hardest travail, that is, he should be a gardener. Delve and dyke, toil and sweat and turn the earth upside down and seek deepness and water the plants in time, and in this he should continue his travail and make sweet floods run and noble plenteous fruits to spring which he should bring before the Lord and serve him there with his desire.

🖙 *Julian of Norwich*, Revelations of Divine Love, fourteenth century

There is no royal road. It is no use asking me or anyone else how to dig – I mean sitting indoors and asking it. Better go and watch a man digging, and then take a spade and try to do it, and go on trying until it comes, and you gain the knack that is to be learnt with all tools, of the doubling of power and halving the effort: and meanwhile you will be learning other things, about your arms and legs and back and perhaps a little robin will come and give you moral support, and at the same time keep a sharp look-out for any worms you may happen to turn up; and you will find out there are all sorts of ways of learning, not only from people and books, but from sheer trying.

ᴥ *Gertrude Jekyll*, Wood and Garden, *1899*

One lesson that I have learned is to plant things well from the start. A good start in life is as important to plants as it is to children: they must develop strong roots in a congenial soil, otherwise they will never make the growth that will serve them richly according to their needs in their adult life.

ᴥ *Vita Sackville-West*, Vita Sackville-West's Garden Book, *1968*

Faire Daffadills, we weep to see
You haste away so soone:
As yet the early-rising Sun
Has not attain'd his Noone.
Stay, Stay,
Untill the hasting day
Has run

But to the even-song;
And, having pray'd together, we
Will goe with you along.

We have short time to stay, as you,
We have as short a Spring;
As quick a growth to meet Decay,
As you, or any thing.
We die,
As your hours doe, and drie
Away,
Like to the Summeres raine;
Or as the pearles of Mornings dew,
Ne'er to be found again.

☙ *Robert Herrick*, 'To Daffadills', *1648*

For the joys a garden brings are already going as
they come. They are poignant. When the first apple
falls with that tremendous thud, one of the big
seasonal changes startles the heart. The swanlike
peony suddenly lets all its petals fall in a snowy pile,
and it is time to say goodbye until another June. But

by then the delphinium is on the way, and the lilies . . . the flowers ring their changes through a long cycle, a cycle that will be renewed. That is what the gardener often forgets. To the flowers we never have to say goodbye forever. We grow older every year, but not the garden; it is reborn every spring.

May Sarton, Plant Dreaming Deep, *1968*

Every morning the day is reborn among the newly blossomed flowers with the same message retold and the same assurance renewed that death eternally dies, that the waves of turmoil are on the surface, and the sea of tranquillity is fathomless.

Rabindranath Tagore, Sadhana, *1916*

Strolling around the garden there is no lack of flower . . . The palest of green shoots are already on the quince trees and the roses are also tentatively pushing forth shoots. Everywhere too the herbaceous plants are thrusting up through the earth.

What all this spells is spring and the renewal of the garden's annual cycle of life into death followed by resurrection. For those that ponder the garden this holds a great mystery . . .

What is life after all but a flower that throws up its leaves from the dark earth into the light, unfurls ever larger until, at its zenith, its petals open in response to the warmth of the sun? But such a blossom also fades and falls, to return once more to the earth from whence it sprang. And so do we. Can anything in life be more beautiful than making such a mirror of the human condition?

☙ *Roy Strong*, The Laskett, *2003*

Love all Creation . . . Love every leaf, and every ray of light. Love the plants. Love the animals. Love everything. If you love everything you will perceive the Divine Mystery in all things. Once you perceive it you will comprehend it better every day. And you will come, at last, to love the whole world with an all-embracing love.

☙ *Fyodor Dostoevsky*, Brothers Karamazov, *1880*

Where would the gardener be if there were no more weeds?

~ *Chuang Tzu*, fourth century BCE

Be grateful for the weeds you have in your mind. Eventually they will enrich your practice . . . We pull the weeds and bury them near the plant to give it nourishment.

~ *Shunryu Suzuki*, 'The Art of Zen Gardening', Garden Design

Seldom is the question asked, What is the relation between the weed and the soil? Perhaps even from our narrow standpoint of direct self-interest, the relation is a useful one . . . soil and the living things in and upon it exist in a relation of interdependence and mutual benefit. Presumably the weed is taking something from the soil: perhaps it is also contributing something to it.

~ *Rachel Carson*, Silent Spring, *1962*

Long live the weeds that overwhelm
My narrow vegetable realm!
The bitter rock, the barren soil
That force the son of man to toil;
All things unholy, marred by curse,
The ugly of the universe.
The rough, the wicked, and the wild
That keep the spirit undefiled.
With these I match my little wit
And earn the right to stand or sit,
Hope, love, create, or drink and die:
These shape the creature that is I.

℞ *Theodore Roethke*, 'Long Live the Weeds', twentieth
century

I always think of my sins when I weed. They grow
apace in the same way and are harder still to get rid
of.

℞ *Helena Rutherford Ely*, A Woman's Hardy Garden,
1903

It's the *doing* it that counts. It's the work itself, the studying, the learning, the contriving, the cherishing, the success, and even the failures.

 ❧ *Elizabeth Sheldon*, Time and the Gardener, 2003

A garden is a sanctuary as well as a creation. It increasingly becomes for me both a spiritual and a physical refuge more transforming than I'd ever imagined it to be. There is the particular kind of happiness – never commented on by poets – which comes from seeing that a shrub you'd once assumed dead, one day has minute specks of green on an otherwise lifeless stick.

 ❧ *M. Osler*, A Breath from Elsewhere, 1998

The cherries in the Heian Shrine were left to the last because they, of all the cherries in Kyoto, were the most beautiful . . . And so . . . picking that moment of regret when the spring sun was about to set, they would pause, a little tired, under the trailing branches, and look fondly at each tree – on

around the lake, by the approach to the bridge, by a
bend in the path, under the eaves of the gallery.
And, until the cherries came the following year,
they would close their eyes and see again the colour
and line of a trailing branch.

🐦 *Junichiro Tanizaki*, The Makioka Sisters, translated
by E. G. Seidensticker, *1957*

For lo, the winter is past, the rain is over and gone;
The flowers appear on the earth, the time of singing
    has come
And the voice of the turtle dove is heard in our
    land.
The fig tree puts forth its figs, and the vines are in
    blossom;
They give forth fragrance.
Arise my love, my fair one, and come away.

🐦 *The Song of Solomon 2:11–13*

You herbs, born at the birth of time
More ancient than the gods themselves.
O Plants, with this hymn I sing to you
Our mothers and our gods.

Most excellent of all are you, O Plants.
Your vassals are the trees.
Let him be subject to your powers
The man who seeks to injure you.

✒ 'Hymn in Praise of Herbs', Rig-Veda (*c.* 2500 BC)

The seasons cannot be hurried. Spring comes, and
the grass grows by itself.

✒ *Jon Zabat-Zinn*, Wherever You Go, There You Are,
1994

Every blade of grass has its Angel that bends over it
and whispers, 'Grow, grow'.

✒ *The Talmud*

Some keep the Sabbath going to Church,
I keep it staying at home –
With a bobolink for a chorister,
And an orchard for a dome –

Some keep the Sabbath in surplice,
I just wear my wings –
And instead of tolling the bell for Church,
Our little sexton sings.

God preaches – a noted Clergyman –
And the sermon is never long,
So instead of getting to heaven at last,
I'm going, all along.

🖎 *Emily Dickinson*, The Complete Poems of Emily
Dickinson, *1924*

As the leaves of the trees are said to absorb all noxious qualities of the air, and to breathe forth a purer atmosphere, so it seems to me as if they drew from us all sordid and angry passions, and breathed forth peace and philanthropy.

🙈 *Washington Irving*, Sketch Book, *1820*

A garden really lives only in so far as it is an expression of faith, the embodiment of a hope and a song of praise.

🙈 *Russell Page*, The Education of a Gardener, *1962*

Don't underestimate the therapeutic value of gardening. It's the one area we can all use our nascent creative talents to make a truly satisfying work of art. Every individual, with thought, patience and a large portion of help from nature, has it in them to create their own private paradise; truly a thing of beauty and a joy for ever.

🙈 *Geoff Hamilton*, Paradise Gardens, *1997*

When in these fresh mornings I go into my garden before anyone is awake, I go for the time being into perfect happiness. In this hour divinely fresh and still, the fair face of every flower salutes me with silent joy that fills me with infinite content; each gives me its color, its grace, its perfume, and enriches me with the consummation of its beauty.

∾ *Celia Thaxter*, An Island Garden, *1894*

A soul who is not close to nature is far away from what is called spirituality. In order to be spiritual one must communicate, and especially one must communicate with nature; one must feel nature.

∾ *Hazrat Inayat Khan*, The Sufi Message: The Art of Personality, *1937*

But a thing that is incarnate with the life of the soul – like the little flower – you can reach out and look into and suddenly find that you are taking hold of the things that lift you up and carry you along and make people love you and give you the joy of life and the joy of living and the joy of having come into the place God has for you, and the exuberance of filling that place in life.

   Henry David Thoreau, Journal, *1859*

People are turning to their gardens not to consume but to actively create, not to escape from reality but to observe it closely. In doing this they experience the connectedness of creation and the profoundest sources of being. That the world we live in and the activity of making it are one seamless whole is something that we may occasionally glimpse. In the garden, we know.

   Carol Williams, Bringing a Garden to Life, *1998*

More than ever I want to see in those blossoms at dawn the god's face.

   Matsuo Basho, seventeenth century

The man who worries night and morning about the dandelions in the lawn will find great relief in loving the dandelions. Each blossom is worth more than a gold coin, as it shines in the exuberant sunlight of the growing spring, and attracts the insects to its bosom . . . Love the things nearest at hand, and love intensely.

ᔗ *Liberty Hyde Bailey*, The Holy Earth, *1925*

While with an eye made quiet by the power
Of harmony, and the deep power of joy,
We see into the life of things.

ᔗ *William Wordsworth*, 'Lines Composed a Few Miles
above Tintern Abbey', *1798*

This outward spring and garden are a reflection of the inward garden.

ᔗ *Mevlana Jalaluddin Rumi*, thirteenth century

Here I am, weeding, snipping and digging, and trying to work out the meaning of it all. I start at one end, and by the time I get to the other it's time to start again. It might seem a strange occupation. But people who think the mundane aspects of gardening are boring don't realize that repetitive garden tasks work like the repeated words of a mantra and free the mind to roam far and wide.

☞ *Jo Munro*, 'A Sense of Place: What's a Garden, Anyway?', Hortus, Spring *1999*

The more one gardens, the more one learns; and the more one learns, the more one realizes how little one knows. I suppose the whole of life is like that: the endless complications, the endless difficulties, the endless fighting against one thing or another, whether it be greenfly on the roses or the complexity of personal relationships.

☞ *Vita Sackville-West*, twentieth century

Last night, there came a frost, which has done great damage to my garden . . . It is sad that Nature will play such tricks on us poor mortals, inviting us with sunny smiles to confide in her, and then, when we are entirely within her power, striking us to the heart.

∾ *Nathaniel Hawthorne*, The American Notebooks, *1883*

It was the month of March, the days were growing longer, winter was departing; winter always carries with it something of our sadness. Then April came, that daybreak of summer, fresh like every dawn, gay like every childhood; weeping a little sometimes like the infant that it is. Nature in this month has charming gleams which pass from the sky, the clouds, the trees, the fields, and the flowers, into the heart of man.

∾ *Victor Hugo*, nineteenth century

A little garden on a bleak hillside
Where deep the heavy, dazzling mountain snow
Lies far into the spring. The sun's pale glow
Is scarcely able to melt patches wide
About the single rose bush. All denied
Of nature's tender ministries. But no, –
For wonder-working faith has made it blow
With flowers many hued and starry-eyed.
Here sleeps the sun long, idle summer hours;
Here butterflies and bees fare far to rove
Amid the crumpled leaves of poppy flowers;
Here four o'clocks, to the passionate night above
Fling whiffs of perfume, like pale incense showers.
A little garden, loved with great love!

     Amy Lowell, 'The Little Garden', twentieth century

But the greatest mystery in the bursting forth of
plants is that it is done when growth is at its tenderest
age; when the shoot is tender and brittle it has power
to push through everything that binds it down.

     Canon Henry Ellacombe, In a Gloucestershire
     Garden, *1895*

What you can do, or dream you can – begin it.
Boldness has genius, power and magic in it.

  🙠 *Johann Wolfgang Goethe*

There is no spot of ground, however arid, bare, or
ugly, that cannot be tamed into such a state as may
give an impression of beauty and delight. It cannot
always be done easily; many things worth doing are
not done easily; but there is no place under natural
conditions that cannot be graced with an
adornment of suitable vegetation.

  🙠 *Gertrude Jekyll*, Home and Garden, *1900*

[In] cyclones of snow and ice, begins the spring.
And such a spring. No wonder that Our Lady
Persephone does not gladly nor promptly come up
again into so ungenial a world as this of ours. The
earth is in agony for her; great rents open and gape
in all directions. The garden is a waste of dark
crumbling clods, and the plants everywhere look

inconceivably dead and hopeless and beyond
thought of resurrection. Only the Tulips and
Daffodils already poke up green noses of vitality;
the Hellebores send up their pale ghosts of blossom
– to be immediately spattered out of shape and
colour by a storm, or else devoured piecemeal by a
slug. Everything else is in the last and lowest hour
of death, shrunk to its smallest proportions, with
the vital principle lurking far down underground
and out of harm's way. And on the dead rose bushes
hang a thousand buds, like withered moths, dark
amid the whirling snow-flakes.

❦ *R. J. Farrer*, In a Yorkshire Garden, *1909*

The tall Tulips would be at their best, *Iris florentina*
and its early companions in full glory. Lilacs and
Apple-blossom, Hawthorn and Laburnum, all
masses of flower. Trees full of tender green, yet not
too densely clad to prevent our seeing the
architecture of the boughs. The Mulberry would be
in leaf and showing that frosts have ceased, for it is

the wisest of all trees, and always waits till it is quite
safe before it opens its buds.

๛ *E. A. Bowles*, My Garden in Spring, *1914*

The earth is at the same time mother,
She is mother of all that is natural, mother of all
that is human,
She is the mother of all, for contained in her
Are the seeds of all.

The earth of humankind
Contains all moistness, all verdancy, all
germinating power.
It is in so many ways fruitful,
All creation comes from it.
Yet it forms not only the basic raw material for
humankind, but also the substance of the
incarnation of God's son.

๛ *Hildegard of Bingen*, twelfth century

Every bird that sings, and every bud that blooms,
does but remind me more of that garden unseen,
awaiting the hand that tills it.

൞ *Emily Dickinson*, letter to Susan Gilbert Dickinson,
   1852

. . . daffodils,
That come before the swallow dares, and take
The winds of March with beauty; violets dim,
But sweeter than the lids of Juno's eyes
Or Cytherea's breath; pale primroses,
That die unmarried, ere they can behold
Bright Phoebus in his strength.

൞ *William Shakespeare*, The Winter's Tale, *IV. iv.118*

My gardens sweet enclosed with walls strong
Embanked with benches to sit and take my rest
The knots so exquisite it cannot be expressed
With arbours and alleys so pleasant and so sweet
The pestilent airs with flavours do repulse.

൞ George Cavendish, The Life and Death of Cardinal
   Wolsey, *c. 1557*

But of the greatest interest is the effect of fragrance on the psychic and mental state of the individual. Powers of perception become clearer and more acute and there is a feeling of having, to a certain extent, outstripped events. They are seen more objectively, and therefore in truer perspective.

 ❧ *Marguerite Maury*, Marguerite Maury's Guide to Aromatherapy, *1989*

Spring is the period
Express from God –
Among the other seasons
Himself abide.

But during March and April
None stir abroad
Without a cordial interview
With God.

 ❧ *Emily Dickinson*, The Complete Poems of Emily Dickinson, *1924*

How astonishing does the chance of leaving the world improve a sense of its natural beauties upon us! . . . I muse with the greatest affection on every flower I have known from my infancy – their shapes and colours are as new to me as if I had just created them with a superhuman fancy. It is because they are connected with the most thoughtless and the happiest moments of our lives. I have seen foreign flowers in hothouses, of the most beautiful nature, but I do not care a straw for them. The simple flowers of our spring are what I want to see again.

☙ *John Keats*, letter to James Rice, *1860*

Come quickly – as soon as
These blossoms open,
They fall.
This world exists
As a sheen of dew on flowers.

☙ *Izumi Shikibu*, eleventh century

If well managed nothing is more beautiful than the kitchen garden: the earliest blossoms come there: we shall in vain seek for flowering shrubs in March, and early April, to equal the peaches, nectarines, apricots, and plums; late in April, we shall find nothing to equal the pear and the cherry; and, in May, the dwarf, or espalier, apple trees, are just so many immense garlands of carnations. The walks are unshaded; they are not greasy or covered with moss, in the spring of the year, like those in the shrubberies; to watch the progress of crops is by no means unentertaining to any rational creature; and the kitchen-garden gives you all this long before the ornamental part of the garden affords you any thing worth looking at.

♌ *William Cobbett*, The English Gardener, *1829*

Don't aim at success – the more you aim at it and make it a target, the more you are going to miss it. For success, like happiness, cannot be pursued; it must ensue . . . as the unintended side-effect of one's personal dedication to a cause greater than oneself . . .

🙠 *Viktor Frankl*, Man's Search for Meaning, written in German 1945, published in English in *1957*

Other species are our kin. This perception is literally true in evolutionary time. All higher eukaryotic organisms, from flowering plants to insects and humanity itself, are thought to have descended from a single ancestral population that lived about 1.8 billion years ago.

🙠 *Edward O. Wilson*, The Biophilia Hypothesis, *1993*

In their native soil, worms are so careful and so gentle. Under the apple trees in the garden the first flakes of blossom are lying; and, after dark, when the dew is falling, and condensing on the white petals, the worms move up their galleries from the lower earth and put out their heads and feel the night air. They listen – not with ears, but with their entire bodies, which are sensitive to light and to all ground vibration. Then, feeling that it is safe, one after another begins to move out of its tunnel, and with eager pointed head, to search for petals of fallen apple-blossom. When a petal is found, it is taken in the worm's mouth and the worm withdraws into the tunnel, and leaves the petal outside the hole . . .

When the worm has, and so carefully, gathered about a dozen petals at the mouth of the tunnel, it picks them up in its mouth, one after the other, and then goes down into the darkness and eats them. Thus the night-wanderer turns blossom into the finest soil or humus, which feeds the roots of the tree once more. Worms are soil-makers; and their galleries and tunnels act as drains to the top-soil. They are poets, choosing at their annual spring festival the choicest food and converting it, after much enjoyment, into food for the trees again. Like poets, they are the natural priests of the earth.

Henry Williamson, Goodbye West Country, *1936*

One day, the Lover took the disciple and told him to dig up a patch of waste ground. When the Lover told him to do this the Disciple was very glad for usually the Lover kept to himself all such hard tasks, and therefore he dug zealously and deep and as he dug he turned up many loathsome worms, slimy and obscene. These, since his heart had grown more gentle than when first he entered the Garden, he collected carefully together in a sack although he much disliked touching them, and carrying them to the edge of the Garden put them beyond its bounds, for it seemed to him intolerable that any such hideous things should deface the glory of the garden of the Beloved.

So when the time came for planting the Garden they sowed seed throughout the Garden where they had dug it, and in due season lovely flowers and green herbs sprung up everywhere save only the plot which the Disciple had dug. This remained bare and barren.

When the Disciple saw this he was very sad and going to the Lover asked him saying, 'Sir, tell me, I pray you, is it my sins that have rendered the plot which I dug barren and yielding no fruit or beauty to the Beloved?'

The Lover answered, 'Tell me carefully all that you did when you dug this plot.'

To which the Disciple replied, 'I put my spade deep into the earth for I was glad of hard toil in the service of the Beloved. Then I turned over the earth with my spade and in it were loathsome worms. These, much as I disliked touching them, I placed in a sack and carried outside the boundary of the garden. For I desired to move such ugliness from the garden of the Beloved.

Then said the Lover, 'These creatures which seemed to you so loathsome are fellow workers with us in the service of the Beloved, for burrowing in the earth they allow air to get to the roots of the plants and they swallow and digest the earth so that the plants can draw nourishment from it, and without their help no plant can grow. So you see indeed these creatures which seem to us so loathsome are in truth more profitable servants to the Beloved than we ourselves.'

The Disciple then asked, 'How can I repair this

great damage which in my ignorance I have done to
the garden?'

The Lover replied, 'Go out of the garden to the
place where you put the worms and dig there so that
you may find these or other worms which you can
bring back to the plot to work for the glory of the
Garden of the Beloved.'

The Disciple went out of the garden though he
much disliked leaving it even for so short a time
and dug and took up the worms and lifting them
very lovingly and with great reverence brought
them to the barren plot which thereafter was barren
no more.

ॐ *Robert Way*, The Garden of the Beloved, *1975*

Nature's object in making animals and plants
might possibly be first of all the happiness of each
one of them, not the creation of all for the
happiness of one. Why ought man to value himself
as more than an infinitely small composing unit of
creation? . . . The universe would be incomplete
without man; but it would also be incomplete

without the smallest transmicroscopic creature that
dwells beyond our conceitful eye and knowledge.

🦢 *John Muir*, nineteenth century

All things must come to the soul from its roots,
from where it is planted. The tree that is beside
running water is fresher and gives more fruit.

🦢 *St Teresa of Avila*, sixteenth century

I cannot say
which is which:
the glowing
plum blossom is
the spring night's moon.

🦢 *Izumi Shikibu*, eleventh century

. . . Gardening is one of the late joys, for youth is
too impatient, too self-absorbed, and usually not
rooted deeply enough to create a garden. Gardening
is one of the rewards of middle age, when one is

ready for an impersonal passion, a passion that demands patience, acute awareness of the world outside oneself, and the power to keep on growing through all the times of drought, through the cold snows, toward those moments of pure joy when all failures are forgotten and the plum tree flowers.

≈ *May Sarton*, Plant Dreaming Deep, *1968*

It's late April. The garden is full of primroses and courting birds. A family of rabbits, out of a touching if foolhardy sense of security in this arcadia, have dug a barrow right underneath the pear tree. Blackie has followed their every move, and now sits at the living-room window eyeing the youngsters. She has no philosophical problems about being a part of nature and apart from nature. The pane of glass, framing her destined booty, causes her neither confusion nor alienation. She doesn't attempt to burst through it, or stalk defeatedly away. She understands its mediating role perfectly. She simply sights up the young rabbits, moves a pace towards the door, slips back to check their position, then hurtles out the cat-flap, round three sides of the house and polishes off another one.

☞ *Richard Mabey*, Nature Cure, 2005

Nature, which governs the whole, will soon change all things which thou seest, and out of their substance will make other things, and again other things from the substance of them, in order that the world may be ever new.

☞ *Marcus Aurelius*, Meditations, 180 AD

The Earth that's Nature's mother is her tomb,
What is her burying grave, that is her womb,
And from her womb children of divers kind
We sucking on her natural bosom find,
Many for many virtues excellent,
None but for some and yet all different.
O mickle is the powerful grace that lies
In plants, herbs, stones and their true qualities

For nought so vile that on the earth doth live
But to the earth some special good doth give.

᠅ *William Shakespeare*, Romeo and Juliet, *II.3.9–18*

We do not really care what we are treading on: we
rush somewhere like mad people and at most
glimpse what beautiful clouds there are up here or
what a beautiful horizon there is back there or what
beautiful mountains; but we do not look beneath
our feet to be able to say and celebrate that the soil
is beautiful here. You should have a garden the size
of a postage stamp; you should have at least one
small flowerbed to learn what you are treading on.
Then you would see, dear boy, that not even clouds
are as varied, beautiful and dreadful as the soil
beneath your feet. You would be able to recognize
soil which is acid, viscid, clayey, cold, stony and
nasty; you would be able to distinguish topsoil as
airy as gingerbread, as warm, light and good as
bread, and you would say that it was beautiful, as
you now say about women or clouds. You would feel
a particular, sensual pleasure as you drove your

stick a yard into the crumbly, friable soil or as you crushed a clod in your fist to sample its airy, moist warmth.

And if you cannot appreciate this singular beauty, then may fate bestow a few square yards of clay upon you as a punishment, clay like tin, substantial, primeval clay, from which a coldness oozes, which will warp under your spade like chewing gum, bake solid in the sun and turn acid in the shade; a clay which is maleficent, unyielding, greasy and kiln-ready, as slippery as a snake and as dry as a brick, as airtight as sheet metal and as heavy as lead. And now break it up with a pick, chop it with a spade, smash it with a hammer, turn it over and cultivate it, cursing loudly and lamenting. Then you will understand what enmity is and the obduracy of inanimate, sterile matter which ever did refuse to become a soil of life and still does now; and you will appreciate what a frightful struggle life must have engaged in, inch by inch, to take hold on the soil of the earth, whether that life be called vegetation or man.

And then you will have to recognize that you

have to give more to the soil than you take from it; you have to break it up and feed it with lime, and heat it with warm manure, sprinkle ashes on it lightly, and flood it with air and sunshine. Then the baked clay begins to fall apart and crumble as if it were breathing quietly; it yields loosely under your spade and with conspicuous willingness; it is warm and pliant in your palm; it is tamed. I tell you, to tame a few yards of soil is a great victory. You do not even think about what you are going to sow in it now. What, is the sight of this dark, airy soil not beautiful enough? Is it not more beautiful than a bed of Pansies or a Carrot patch? You almost envy the vegetation which is going to take possession of this noble, human achievement called topsoil.

And from this time on you will not walk over the earth again not knowing what you are treading on.

  Karel Čapek, The Gardener's Year, *1929*

The thin layer of soil that forms a patchy covering over the continents controls our own existence and that of every other animal of the land. Without soil, land plants as we know them could not grow, and without plants no animals could survive.

. . . it is equally true that soil depends on life, its very origins and the maintenance of its true nature being intimately related to living plants and animals. For soil is in part a creation of life, born of a marvellous interaction of life and non-life aeons ago . . . Life not only formed the soil, but other living things of incredible abundance and diversity now exist within it; if this were not so the soil would be a dead and sterile thing. By their presence and by their activities the myriad organisms of the soil make it capable of supporting the earth's green mantle.

The soil exists in a state of constant change, taking part in cycles that have no beginning and no end. New materials are constantly being contributed as rocks disintegrate, as organic matter decays, and as nitrogen and other gases are brought down in rain from the skies. At the same time other materials are being taken away, borrowed for temporary use by living creatures. Subtle and vastly important chemical changes are constantly in progress, converting elements derived from air and water into forms suitable for use by plants. In all these changes living organisms are active agents . . .

[The soil community – bacteria, fungi and algae, mites and earthworms –] consists of a web of interwoven lives, each in some way related to the others – the living creatures depending on the soil, but the soil in turn a vital element of the earth only so long as this community within it flourishes.

Rachel Carson, Silent Spring, *1968*

There is no essential definition of a garden; a garden needn't have any plant material at all. But most gardens do, and accordingly they make statements about our place in and relation to nature. Buildings do enclose us, but they do not, in addition, as do most gardens, make us think about wilderness, other species, interdependence, the passage of time, the limits of control.

Stephanie Ross, What Gardens Mean, *1998*

I must tell you one day what these trees came to mean to me – particularly the birches, and the mountain ash with its flashes of colour memorialising my native land. As it took root and pushed out its first timid foliage I began to see it and the wheatfield above as my totems of place. I planted the tree as a way of leaving something living behind me. Trees are not eternal stone, but they remind us that stone had once been living fire, and sometimes served, while it cooled, as flowerpress, seedbed . . . Just as stone will outlast us, our trees, too, will outlive the fragile traces we make such a show of leaving in our names. Meanwhile the leaves may bud and flourish and sear and fall, and birds may find a home in their branches.

    Robert Walshe, Wales' Work, *1986*

It may be that some little root of the sacred tree still lives. Nourish it then, that it may leaf and bloom and fill with singing birds.

    Black Elk, twentieth century

Do not occupy your precious time except with the most precious of things, and the most precious of human things is the state of being occupied between the past and the future.

ᔒ *Ahmed b. Isa al-Kharraz*, ninth century

In pale moonlight
The wisteria scent
Comes from far away.

ᔒ *Buson*, eighteenth century

I go down into the cellar to find dahlia tubers from the fall. They are wizened ugly things. I can hardly believe these brown and wrinkled lumps of matter are going to be flowers . . .

I spade up a place in the bank for each tuber. In they go! I replace the earth. I do not have to sweat. The dahlias know what to do. Leaves will come. Flowers will come. Some years they will even be profuse. Then the dahlias will die. I will dig up the tubers. I will put them in the cellar. And they will be planted again the following year if all things remain the same . . .

Can I live this dahlia way too? A way that does not complicate, does not avoid, or force things to happen. A direct way that simply opens ... allowing for process? To plant, to flower in the sun, and to surrender to the frost when it comes, this way is thorough. It occurs in every aspect of life and skips nothing. It is living and dying, again and again. It is so simple, this allowing, and so profound.

🔻 *Gunilla Norris*, Journeying in Place: Reflections from a Country Garden, *1994*

Our minds should be free from traces of the past, just like the flowers of the spring.

🔻 *Shunryu Suzuki*, twentieth century

Summer

As spring glides seamlessly into summer, gardens put on a dizzying spurt of growth and it's a joy to spend more time outside once again, revelling in the warmth of the sun. We marvel at early summer's beneficence, admiring the jewel-like brilliance of iris and peony, or the old-fashioned cottage garden flowers like Canterbury bells and sweet williams, and inhale the sweet scents of lilac, honeysuckle and philadelphus, as well as freshly mown grass.

We have to contend with fast-growing weeds however, and if we're not disciplined about removing them, they can soon take over, and plants will struggle to give of their best. It can feel like a constant battle, and it's easy to get discouraged, especially if we go away, for our return means a redoubling of effort. Little and often is the best policy, as it is with so many tasks, and it can then be quite therapeutic. Any time spent communing with nature enhances life, and if we concentrate fully on the task in hand, the mental chatter that so often exhausts us, ceases, and we feel refreshed and content when we go indoors.

With the explosion of growth that summer brings, we need to pay attention to everything that's happening in the garden. As we observe, we see what needs to be done, and we learn through doing. Seedlings need to be watered, plants need to be staked, dead flowers have to be removed to encourage further flowering, and shrubs that have finished their cycle of blossoming need to be pruned. There are so many demands on our time, but it's a delicate balancing act between doing what has to be done and taking time to stand and stare – or better still, to sit and watch. Butterflies dance, dragonflies hover and bees hum merrily, seeking out the brightest flowers. We can have a glimpse of eternity if we just stop to admire and smell the roses.

Midsummer is the time when roses are at the height of perfection, first the climbers, then the floribundas and hybrid teas not far behind, vibrating with colour and perfume. While our senses of sight and smell are aroused, so too is our sense of touch, soft petals feeling silky to our fingertips. And, in gazing into the centre of a newly opened rose, we appreciate the wonder of form. Momentarily we can be transported into another realm, as mind, body and spirit are united with nature. When we smell a rose, its fragrance enters the nose with our breath and travels to the limbic system of the brain, the emotional centre. There is also a physiological effect on the nervous system. The use of colour and scent in the garden can be beneficial today as it was in the past, when men and women automatically used colourful and aromatic plants for healing, both of mind and emotions, as well as in physical remedies. The essential oil distilled from rose has a relaxing effect, helps alleviate depression and is also an aphrodisiac. Other plants and flowers like geranium, lavender, heliotrope, clary sage and jasmine can all help reduce anxiety. And basil, pine and rosemary are excellent stimulants. Different colours can also affect our emotional and psychological state. We feel calmed by soft pinks, mauves and blue, and energised by the vibrant colours of red, orange and yellow. White flowers can sing out on a sunny day, but in the moonlight have an ethereal quality. And can anything make us feel cooler and more tranquil on a hot summer's day than an expanse of green lawn and the dappled shade of green foliage?

All five senses are enhanced by summer. Apart from the visual excitement of form and colour, the headiness of aroma, and the texture of petals and leaves that are pleasing to touch, there are the sounds of birds and insects, the rustling of leaves in the breeze, and perhaps the trickle of water to enchant our ears. Then there is nothing to beat the taste of early vegetables like asparagus, broad beans and the salad crops, or lush fruits like ripe strawberries. Fresh food, herbs and aromatics from the garden can nurture both body and soul, and help us feel more closely connected to nature.

Our spirits soar at all this magnificence, and the halcyon days of high summer seem as if they will last forever. In reality they are over in a flash. Everything that blooms in our gardens is over so quickly – nothing is a more poignant reminder of the passing of time. But that in itself reminds us of the importance of living in the present moment and making the most of life's rich offerings.

At the height of summer we may find ourselves longing for rain, as heat becomes excessive and humidity uncomfortable. Endless running around with watering-cans filled from water butts becomes tedious, but a summer thunderstorm can be most welcome, reviving us and having a visible effect in refreshing trees and plants.

All too soon it is late summer, when gardens can be less interesting unless care has been taken to ensure planting of colourful phlox, Japanese anemones, late fuchsias, penstemons, dahlias and agapanthus, while nicotiana can provide some delightful evening fragrance as well as colour. The vegetable garden is a profusion of crops and the fruit trees are burgeoning with their offerings. The cycle of blossoming and fruition has reached its peak.

What greater delight is there than to behold the earth apparelled with plants as with a robe of embroidered work set with orient pearls and garnished with great diversity of rare and costly jewels? . . . But these delights are in the outward senses – the principal delight is in the mind singularly enriched with the knowledge of these visible things, setting forth to us the invisible wisdom and admirable workmanship of almighty God.

ॐ *John Gerard*, The Herball, *1597*

What is one to say about [summertime] – the fulfilment of the promise of the earlier months, and with as yet no sign to remind one that its fresh young beauty will ever fade? . . . The soft cooing of the wood-dove, the glad song of many birds, the flitting of butterflies, the hum of all the little winged people among the branches, the sweet earth-scents — all seem to say the same, with an endless reiteration, never wearying because so gladsome. It is the offering of the Hymn of Praise! The lizards run in and out of the heathy tufts in the hot sunshine, and as the long day darkens the night-jar trolls out his strange song, so welcome because it is the prelude to the perfect summer night . . .

୬ *Gertrude Jekyll*, Wood and Garden, *1899*

A route of evanescence
With a revolving wheel;
A resonance of emerald;
A rush of cochineal.
And every blossom on the bush
Adjusts its tumbled head, —
The mail from Tunis, probably,
An easy morning's ride.

୬ *Emily Dickinson*, Collected Poems of Emily
  Dickinson, *1924*

Every blade of grass, each leaf, each separate floret
and petal, is an inscription speaking of hope . . . So
that my hope becomes as broad as the horizon afar,
reiterated by every leaf, sung on every bough,
reflected in the gleam of every flower.

✍ *Richard Jefferies*, 'The Pageant of Summer',
    Longman's Magazine, June *1883*

A morning glory at my window satisfies me more
than the metaphysics of books.

✍ *Walt Whitman*, 'Song of Myself', *1855*

But it was the blue Ipomée that really made her
heart stand still. When she was a little girl she had
loved to grow 'morning glories', and she had been
encouraged to do so because it got her out of bed in
good time. If you didn't look at them before
breakfast you probably didn't see them at all, and
the best of them faded by the middle of the
morning . . . So that when she saw this Dawn
Flower of the French Riviera for the first time, she

could hardly contain herself. It rioted over everything, as though someone had torn great masses out of a morning sky. It was so blue that it positively hurt. She felt that the heart was being drowned in loveliness, and she could scarcely breathe.

✧ *Reginald Arkell*, Old Herbaceous, *1950*

. . . All the wars of the world, all the Caesars, have not the staying power of a Lily in a cottage border: man creates the storms in his teacup, and dies of them, but there remains a something standing outside, a something impregnable, as far beyond reach of man's destructiveness as is man's own self. The immortality of marbles and of miseries is a vain, small thing compared to the immortality of a flower that blooms and is dead by dusk.

✧ *R. J. Farrer*, The Rainbow Bridge, *1926*

A garden is a sort of sanctuary, a chamber roofed by heaven . . . to wander in, to cherish, to dream through undisturbed . . . a little plesaunce of the soul, by whose wicket the world can be shut out.

 Sir Robert Lorimer, On Scottish Gardens, *1898*

There is probably nothing that has such tranquillizing effect, and leads into such content, as gardening. In half an hour I can hoe myself right away from this world.

 Charles Dudley Warner, My Summer in a Garden, *1873*

What grows in a garden is not just plants but the human spirit itself.

 Matthew Fox, twentieth century

Cut grass lies frail:
Brief is the breath
Mown stalks exhale.
Long, long the death.

It dies in the white hours
Of young-leafed June
With chestnut flowers,
With hedges snowlike strewn.

White lilac bowed
Lost lanes of Queen Anne's lace,
And that high-builded cloud
Moving at summer's pace.

၈ *Philip Larkin*, 'Cut Grass', *1971*

The best remedy for those who are afraid, lonely or unhappy is to go outside where they can be quiet, alone with the heavens, nature and God.

Because only then does one feel that all is as it should be and that God wishes to see people happy, amidst the simple beauty of nature . . .

As long as this exists, and it certainly always
will, I know that there will always be comfort for
every sorrow, whatever the circumstances may be.
And I firmly believe that nature brings solace in all
troubles.

🙠 *Anne Frank*, Diary of a Young Girl, *1944*

The richness I achieve comes from Nature, the
source of my inspiration.

🙠 *Claude Monet*, twentieth century

My garden is surrounded by cornfields and
meadows, and beyond are great stretches of sandy
heath and pine forests, and where the forests leave
off the bare heath begins again; but the forests are
beautiful in their lofty, pine-stemmed vastness, for
overhead the crowns of softest gray-green, and
underfoot a bright green whortleberry carpet, and
everywhere the breathless silence; and the bare
heaths are beautiful too, for one can see across
them into eternity almost, and to go out on to them

with one's face towards the setting sun is like going into the very presence of god . . .

∽ *Elizabeth von Arnim*, Elizabeth and Her German Garden, *1930*

We've worked hard to exile ourselves from nature, yet we end up longing for what we've lost: a sense of connectedness . . . By retreating farther and farther from nature, we lose our sense of belonging, suffer a terrible loneliness we can't name, and end up depriving ourselves of what we need to feel healthy and whole.

∽ *Diane Ackerman*, Cultivating Delight: A Natural History of My Garden, *2001*

A really long day of weeding is a restful experience, and quite changes the current of thought. For some people it is more efficient than a rest cure.

∽ *Anna Lee Merritt*, An Artist's Garden, *1908*

Weeding is a delightful occupation, especially after summer rain, when the roots come up clear and clean. One gets to know how many and various are the ways of weeds – as many almost as the moods of human creatures.

🖎 *Gertrude Jekyll*, Wood and Garden, *1899*

The glory of gardening: hands in the dirt, head in the sun, heart with nature. To nurture a garden is to feed not just the body, but the soul. Share the botanical bliss of gardeners through the ages, who have cultivated philosophies to apply to their own – and our own – lives. Show me your garden and I shall tell you what you are.

🖎 *Alfred Austin*, The Garden that I Love, *1894*

My garden, that skirted the avenue of the Manse, was of precisely the right extent. An hour or two of morning labor was all that it required. But I used to visit and revisit it a dozen times a day, and stand in deep contemplation over my vegetable progeny with a love that nobody could share or conceive of, who had never taken part in the process of creation.

Nathaniel Hawthorne, Mosses from an Old Manse, *1854*

When [the Paeony] finally drops from the vase, it sheds its vast petticoats with a bump on the table, all in an intact heap, much as a rose will suddenly fall, making us look up from our book or conversation, to notice for one moment the death of what had appeared to be a living beauty.

Vita Sackville-West, Vita Sackville-West's Garden Book, *1968*

It does not astonish us or make us angry that it takes a whole year to bring into the house three great white peonies and two pale blue iris. It seems altogether right and appropriate that these glories are earned with long patience and faith . . . and also that it is altogether right and appropriate that they cannot last. Yet in our human relations we are

outraged when the supreme moments, the
moments of flowering, must be waited for . . . and
then cannot last. We reach a summit, and then we
have to go down again.

   May Sarton, Journal of a Solitude, *1973*

White peonies blooming along the porch
Send out light
While the rest of the yard grows dim.

Outrageous flowers as big as human
heads! They're staggered
by their own luxuriance: I had
to prop them up with stakes and twine.
The moist air intensifies their scent,
And the moon moves around the barn
To find out what it's coming from.

In the darkening June evening
I draw a blossom near, and bending close
Search it as a woman searches
A loved one's face.

   Jane Kenyon, 'Peonies at Dusk', *1996*

I think that if ever a mortal heard the voice of God
it would be in a garden at the cool of the day.

F. Frankfurt Moore, A Garden of Peace, *1920*

A garden is a lovesome thing, God wot!
Rose plot,
Fringed pool,
Ferned grot –
The veriest school of peace: and yet the fool
Contends that God is not –
Not God! In gardens! When the eve is cool?
Nay, but I have a sign;
'Tis very sure God walks in mine.

T. E. Brown, 'My Garden', *1893*

A garden enclosed is my sister, my spouse, a
spring shut up, a fountain sealed.
    Thy plants are an orchard of pomegranates,
with pleasant fruits; camphire, with spikenards,
    Spikenard and saffron; calamus and cinnamon,

with all trees of frankincense; myrrh and aloes,
with all the chief spices:

A fountain of gardens, a well of living waters,
and streams from Lebanon.

Awake, O north wind; and come, thou south;
blow upon my garden, that the spices thereof may
flow out. Let my beloved come into his garden, and
eat his pleasant fruits.

✒ Song of Solomon 4:12–16

What shall I learn of beans or beans of me? I
cherish them, I hoe them, early and late I have an
eye to them; and this is my day's work.

✒ Henry David Thoreau, Walden, 1854

I remember people coming to my mother's yard to
be given cuttings from her flowers: I hear again the
praise showered on her because whatever rocky soil
she landed on, she turned into a garden . . . She is
involved in work her soul must have. Ordering the

85

universe in the image of her personal conception of Beauty.

🙠 *Alice Walker*, In Search of Our Mothers' Gardens, *1983*

Often I hear people say, 'How do you make your plants flourish like this?' as they admire the little flower patch I cultivate in summer . . . 'I can never make my plants blossom like this! What is your secret?' And I answer with one word, 'Love'.

🙠 *Celia Thaxter*, An Island Garden, *1894*

It was one of the most bewitching sights in the world to observe a hill of beans thrusting aside the soil, or a row of early peas just peeping forth sufficiently to trace a line of delicate green. Later in the season the hummingbirds were attracted by the blossoms of a peculiar variety of bean; and they were a joy to me, those little spiritual visitants, for deigning to sip airy food out of my nectar-cups.

Multitudes of bees used to bury themselves in the yellow blossoms of the summer-squashes. This too, was a deep satisfaction, although, when they had laden themselves with sweets, they flew away to some unknown hive, which would give back nothing in requital of what my garden had contributed. But I was glad to fling a benefaction upon the passing breeze with the certainty that somebody would profit by it, and that there would be a little more honey in the world to allay the sourness and bitterness which mankind is always complaining of.

➤ *Nathaniel Hawthorne*, Mosses from an Old Manse, *1854*

When we reached them we forgot all our troubles, so singular is the appearance of that called the Beautiful Island (Isola Bella). Imagine a quantity of arcades, formed in the centre of the lake, supporting a conical-shaped hill, cut in four sides, covered with thirty-six terraces, one over the other, nine on each side . . . Each of these terraces is hung with palisades of jessamine, orange trees, or pomegranates, with pots of flowers placed on the ledge.

☞ *Charles de Brosses*, Lettres écrites d'Italie à quelques amis, eighteenth century

Strawberry Hill, June 10, 1765. Eleven at night. I am just come out of the garden in the most oriental of evenings, and from breathing odours beyond those of Araby. The acacias, which the Arabians have the sense to worship, are covered with blossoms, the honeysuckles dangle from every tree in festoons, the seringas are thickets of sweets, and the new-cut hay in the field tempers the balmy gales with simple freshness; while a thousand sky-rockets launched into the air at Ranelagh or Marylebone illuminate the scene, and give it an air of Haroun Alraschid's paradise.

☞ *Horace Walpole*, The Letters of Horace Walpole, *1926*

Sunlight,
Three marigolds,
And a dusky, purple poppy-pod –
Out of these I made a beautiful world.

🌱 *Amy Lowell*, twentieth century

Arranging a bowl of flowers in the morning can
give a sense of quiet in a crowded day – like writing
a poem or saying a prayer.

🌱 *Anne Morrow Lindbergh*, twentieth century

I've noticed something about gardening. You set
out to do one thing and pretty soon you're doing
something else, which leads to some other thing,
and so on. By the end of the day, you look at the
shovel stuck in the half-dug rose bed and wonder
what on earth you've been doing.

You've been gardening, an activity that doesn't
necessarily lead to its supposed goal. This used to
bother me, until I realized that this meandering – a
kind of free association between earth, tools, body
and mind – is the essence of gardening. What is

supposed to be a practical, goal-oriented activity is
actually an act of meditation.

✎ *Anne Raver*, Deep in the Green, *1995*

[F]low is] the state in which people are so involved
in an activity that nothing else seems to matter; the
experience itself is so enjoyable that people will do
it even at great cost, for the sheer sake of doing it.

✎ *Mihaly Csikszentmihalyi*, Flow, *1992*

The rapturous nightingale sings
Wooing the rose
In the midst of the Garden newborn
But only the gardener knows
Of the labour that brings
To the Garden its beauty; he toiled all day in the
heat
And his feet
Have been wounded by many a thorn.

✎ *The Diwan* (Collection of Poems) of Zeb-un-Nissa,
    seventeenth century

Oh, Adam was a gardener, and God who made him
    sees
That half a proper gardener's work is done upon his
    knees,
So when your work is finished, you can wash your
    hands and pray
For the Glory of the Garden, that it may not pass
    away!
And the Glory of the Garden it shall never pass away.

🙠 *Rudyard Kipling*, 'The Glory of the Garden', *1911*

After this he led them into his garden, where was
great variety of flowers; and he said, do you see all
these? So Christiana said, Yes. Then said he again,
Behold the flowers are diverse in stature, in quality,
and colour, and smell and virtue, and some are
better than others; also, where the gardener hath
set them, there they stand, and quarrel not with one
another.

🙠 *John Bunyan*, The Pilgrim's Progress, *1678*

'Flowers and trees,' she said, 'do not speak, but they do have hearts and spirits just like you and me. They can feel your love, hear your heart's message. And "we" the guardians, were created to remind all things of their relationship, and to never forget Earth Mother. She is a living thing – very, very important in the Great Creation of the Great Spirit.'

∽ *Tony Shearer*, The Praying Flute: Song of the Earth, *1991*

The sound of summer is everywhere . . . a faint resonance seems to come from the very earth itself. The fervour of the sunbeams descending in a tidal flood rings on the strung harp of the earth. It is this exquisite undertone, heard and yet unheard, which brings the mind into sweet accordance with the wonderful instrument of nature.

∽ *Richard Jefferies*, 'The Pageant of Summer', Longman's Magazine, *1883*

Garbage becomes rose
Rose becomes compost –
Everything is in transformation.
Even permanence is impermanent.

⊷ *Thich Nhat Hanh*, The Miracle of Mindfulness,
1996

Nevertheless the flowers fall with our attachment,
and the weeds spring up with our aversion.

⊷ *Dogen*, thirteenth century

Let no one think that real gardening is a bucolic
and meditative occupation. It is an insatiable
passion, like everything else to which a man gives
his heart.

⊷ *Karel Čapek*, The Gardener's Year, 1929

Making a garden is not a gentle hobby for the elderly, to be picked up and laid down like a game of solitaire. It is a grand passion. It seizes a person whole, and once it has done so he will have to accept that his life is going to be radically changed. There are seasons when he will hesitate to travel, and if he does travel, his mind will be distracted by the thousand and one children he has left behind, children who are always in peril of one sort or another. However sober he may have been before, he will soon become an inveterate gambler who cuts his losses and begins again; he may think he intends to pare down on spending energy and money, but that is an illusion, and he soon learns that a garden is an ever-expanding venture.

☙ *May Sarton*, Plant Dreaming Deep, *1968*

The principal value of a private garden . . . is not to give the possessor vegetables and fruit . . . but to teach him patience and philosophy, and the higher virtues — hope deferred and expectations blighted.

☙ *Charles Dudley Warner*, My Summer in a Garden, *1870*

I long to accomplish a great and noble task, but it is
my chief duty to accomplish small tasks as if they
were great and noble.

   ✒ *Helen Keller*, twentieth century

If it were any use, every day the gardener would
fall on his knees and pray somehow like this:
'O Lord, grant that in some way it may rain every
day, say from about midnight until 3 o'clock in
the morning, but, you see, it must be gentle and
warm so that it can soak in; grant that at the same
time it would not rain on campion, alyssum,
helianthemum, lavender, and others which you
in your infinite wisdom know are drought-loving
plants – I will write their names on a bit of paper
if you like – and grant that the sun may shine
the whole day long, but not everywhere (not, for
instance, on spiraea, or on gentian, plantain
lily, and rhododendron), and not too much;
that there may be plenty of dew and little wind,
enough worms, no plant lice and snails, no

mildew, and that once a week thin liquid manure
and guano may fall from heaven. Amen.'

☙ *Karel Čapek*, The Gardener's Year, *1929*

Be still, my soul. Consider
The flowers and the stars.
Among these sleeping fragrances,
Sleep now your cares.
That which the universe
Lacks room to enclose
Lives in the folded petals
Of this dark rose.

☙ *Gerald Bullett*, 'In the Garden at Night', twentieth
century

Nobody sees a flower really – it is so small it takes
time – we haven't time – and to see takes time, like
to have a friend takes time.

☙ *Georgia O'Keefe*, twentieth century

When we look into the heart of a flower, we see clouds, sunshine, minerals, time, the earth, and everything else in the cosmos in it. Without clouds, there could be no rain, and there would be no flower. Without time the flower could not bloom. In fact, the flower is made entirely of non-flower elements; it has not independent, individual existence . . .

Thich Nhat Hahn, twentieth century

Ah, these jasmines, these white jasmines!
I seem to remember the first day when I filled my hands with these jasmines, these white jasmines.

I have loved the sunlight, the sky and the green earth; I have heard the liquid murmur of the river through the darkness of midnight . . .

Yet my heart is sweet with the memory of the first fresh jasmines that filled my hands when I was a child.

Rabindranath Tagore, 'The First Jasmines', The Crescent Moon, *1913*

A flower's fragrance declares to all the world that it is fertile, available, and desirable, its sex organs oozing with nectar. Its smells remind us in vestigial ways of fertility, vigor, life-force, all the optimism, expectancy and passionate bloom in youth. We inhale its ardent aroma and, no matter what our ages, we feel young and nubile in a world aflame with desire.

   Diane Ackerman, A Natural History of the Senses, *1990*

Lady butterfly
Perfumes her wings
By floating
Over the orchid

   Matsuo Basho, seventeenth century

Through the open door
A drowsy smell of flowers – gray heliotrope
And white sweet clover, and shy mignonette
Comes faintly in, and silent chorus leads
To the pervading symphony of peace.

John Greenleaf Whittier, nineteenth century

I do wander everywhere
Swifter than the moon's sphere;
And I serve the fairy queen,
To dew her orbs upon the green.
The cowslips tall her pensioners be:
In their gold coats spots you see;
There be rubies, fairy favours,
In those freckles live their savours.
I must go seek some dew-drops here,
And hang a pearl in every cowslip's ear.

William Shakespeare, A Midsummer Night's
Dream, *II.1.6–15*

A garden full of sweet odors is a garden full of charm, a most precious kind of charm not to be implanted by mere skill in horticulture or power of purse, and which is beyond explaining. It is born of sensitive and very personal preferences yet its appeal is almost universal. Fragrance speaks to many to whom color and form say little, and it 'can bring irresistibly as music emotions of all sorts to the mind'.

> ꙮ *Louise Beebe Wilder*, The Fragrant Path, *1932*

When you feel out of sorts or mad at the world, turn to the warm generosity and friendliness of your garden. You will find it ever so full of joy and gaiety, colour and beauty, and all the things that go to making a full and cheerful life – you will find contentment and happiness. Your garden is your playground, and the best room in your house. The pride, interest, and delight you will gain by making it a place of colourful splendour will banish your troubles as quickly as the rising sun dispels the morning mist. So, turn to nature, step into the garden, and out into the sun . . .

   🙠 Colour Fragrance for the Winter Garden, *c. 1960*,
      pamphlet, Anderson & Co.

The whole garden is singing [a] hymn of praise and thankfulness . . . by bedtime rain was falling . . . It was pleasant to wake from time to time and hear the welcome sound, and to know that the clogged leaves were being washed clean, and that their pores were once more drawing in the breath of life, and that the thirsty roots were drinking their fill. And now, in the morning, how good it is to see the brilliant light of the blessed summer day, always brightest just after rain, and to see how every tree and plant is full of new life and abounding gladness; and to feel one's own thankfulness of heart, and that it is good to live, and all the more good to live in a garden.

   🙠 *Gertrude Jekyll*, Home and Garden, *1900*

The watering of a garden requires nearly as much judgement as the seasoning of a soup.

↪ *Mrs Helena Rutherford Ely*, A Woman's Hardy Garden, *1903*

If God created the earth, so is the earth beloved; and if it is hallowed, so must we deal with it devotedly and with care that we do not despoil it, and mindful of our relations to all beings that live on it. We are to consider it religiously: Put off thy shoes from thy feet, for the place wheron thou standest is holy ground.

↪ *Liberty Hyde Bailey*, The Holy Earth, *1925*

When once the sun sinks in the west,
And dewdrops pearl the evening's breast;
Almost as pale as moonbeams are,
Or its companionable star,
The evening primrose opens anew
Its delicate blossoms to the dew;
And, hermit-like, shunning the light,

Wastes its fair bloom upon the night,
Who, blindfold to its fond caresses,
Knows not the beauty it possesses;
Thus it blooms on while night is by;
When day looks out with open eye,
Bashed at the gaze it cannot shun,
It faints and withers and is gone.

John Clare, 'Evening Primrose', *1835*

Evidence now supports the vision of the poet and
the philosopher that plants are living, breathing,
communicating creatures, endowed with
personality and the attributes of soul.

Peter Tompkins and Christopher Bird, The Secret Life
of Plants, *1973*

If we have flowers, are we not 'born again' every
day . . .

Emily Dickinson, letter to Mrs George S.
Dickinson, *1886*

Although colour and aroma have a profound influence on our physical well-being, increasingly we are realizing that these are not only physical forces but spiritual ones which have a profound effect on all aspects of our being.

꩜ *Suzy Chiazzari*, Colour Scents: Healing with Colour and Aroma, *1998*

You turn and see, where the glade opens out . . . a grey stone wall. In front of the wall is colour – that is what you see, not flowers, not stems and leaves and petals, but simply a block of pure colour, the most heart-stopping, astonishing blue, the blue of a Mediterranean sky or the Aegean Sea in late afternoon, the blue of lapis lazuli, blended with smoky violet. Irises, planted in a broad band along the wall, irises as you have never seen them. The sight arouses not just delight and admiration, it arouses a kind of greed within you. You <u>want</u> that colour. Your desire for it is passionate and it startles you; you could not have imagined that such a feeling could be stirred by flowers in a garden.

But as you pull yourself away and walk bemusedly
back . . . perhaps it dawns on you that you
recognize your feelings — you know them well
enough. Most people do. You have fallen in love,
though not with a person, with a garden.

᠊ᡂ *Susan Hill and Rory Stuart*, Reflections from a
      Garden, *1995*

Narrow paths between high, built-up banks
supporting flower borders, crowded with jonquils,
auriculas, forget-me-nots and other spring flowers,
led from one part of the garden to another. One
winding path led to the earth closet in its bower of
nut-trees halfway down the garden, another to the
vegetable garden and on to the rough grass plot
before the beehives. Between each section were
thick groves of bushes with ferns and capers and
Solomon's seal, so closed in that the long, rough
grass there was always damp. Wasted ground, a good
gardener might have said, but delightful in its cool,
green shadiness.

 Nearer the house was a portion given up

entirely to flowers, not growing in beds or borders, but crammed together in an irregular square, where they bloomed in half-wild profusion. There were rose bushes there and lavender and rosemary and a bush apple-tree which bore little red and yellow streaked apples in later summer, and Michaelmas daisies and red-hot pokers and old-fashioned pompom dahlias in autumn and peonies and pinks already budding.

✍ *Flora Thompson*, Lark Rise to Candleford, *1939*

I judge a garden by the gardener who cares for it, the one who invests space with daydreams. What is a garden but a species of desire? How well I know the downward gaze into the face of the earth, the feelings of a luxurious body in good, dark soil that slips through the fingers in the rush to return to its dirty delirium. Each gardener creates an ideal world of miniature thoughts that drift languidly into each other like flowers on a dry afternoon. Here silence has the rhythm of wishes.

Gardens have that special resistance beautiful

things offer to our understanding. Some days I think it is enough to watch a hummingbird wander into the sweet tunnel of a trumpet vine climbing up a summer sky. Maybe gardening is a form of worship.

❧ *Bonnie Marranca*, American Garden Writing, *1988*

A something in a summer's day,
As slow her flambeaux burn away,
Which solemnizes me.

A something in a summer's noon –
An azure depth, a wordless tune,
Transcending ecstasy.

And still within a summer's night
A something so transporting bright,
I clap my hands to see.

❧ *Emily Dickinson*, The Complete Poems of Emily
    Dickinson, *1924*

In the window . . . there is a scarlet geranium shining with its scarlet tops in the sun, the red of it being the more red for a background of lime-trees which are at the same time breathing and panting like airy plenitudes of joy, and developing their shifting depths of light and shade, of russet browns and sunny inward gold.

It seems to say, 'Paint me!' so here it is . . . and upon looking closer at the flowers, we observe that some of the petals are transparent with the light, while others are left in the shade; the leaves are equally adorned, after their opaquer fashion, with those effects of the sky, showing their dark brown rims; and on one of them a red petal has fallen, where it lies on the brighter half of the shallow green cup, making its own red redder, and the green greener. We perceive, in imagination, the scent of those good-natured leaves, which allow you to carry off their perfume on your fingers; for good natured they are in that respect . . .

☙ *Leigh Hunt*, 'A Flower for Your Window', in The Seer, or Common-Places Refreshed, *1840*

Care of the soul requires craft . . . skill, attention, and art. To live with a high degree of artfulness means to attend to the small things that keep the soul engaged in whatever we are doing, and it is the very heart of soul-making. From some grand overview of life, it may seem that only the big events are ultimately important. But to the soul, the most minute details and the most ordinary activities, carried out with mindfulness and art, have an effect far beyond their apparent insignificance.

Thomas Moore, Care of the Soul, *1992*

. . . Here's flowers for you:
Hot lavender, mints, savory, marjoram;
The marigold, that goes to bed wi' the sun,
And with him rises weeping . . .

William Shakespeare, The Winter's Tale, *IV.iv.103*

As I work among my flowers, I find myself talking to them, reasoning and remonstrating with them, and adoring them as if they were human beings.

🖎 *Celia Thaxter*, An Island Garden, *1894*

Plants can change our state of mind, alter our consciousness or evoke an energy or deity from the world of spirit.

🖎 *Pamela Woods*, Gardens for the Soul, *2002*

In a fine extensive garden or park an Englishman expects to see a number of groves and glades, intermingled with agreeable negligence, which seems to be the effect of nature and accident. He looks for shady walks encrusted with gravel; for open lawns covered with verdure as smooth as velvet, but much more lively and agreeable; for ponds, canals, basins, cascades and running streams of water; for clumps of trees, woods and wildernesses, cut into delightful alleys, perfumed with honeysuckle and sweet-briar, and resounding with the mingled melody of all the singing birds of heaven; he looks for plots of flowers in different parts to refresh the sense, and please the fancy; for arbours, grottos, hermitages, temples and alcoves, to shelter him from the sun, and afford him means of contemplation and repose; and he expects to find the hedges, groves, and walks, and lawns kept with the utmost order and propriety . . .

Tobias Smollett, Travels through France and Italy, 1766

So, some tempestuous morn in early June,
When the year's primal burst of bloom is o'er,
Before the roses and the longest day —
When garden-walks and all the grassy floor
With blossoms red and white of fallen May
And chestnut-flowers are strewn —
So have I heard the cuckoo's parting cry,
From the wet field, through the vext garden-trees
Come with the volleying rain and tossing breeze:
The bloom is gone, and with the bloom go I.

Too quick despairer, wherefore wilt thou go?
Soon will the high Midsummer pomps come on,
Soon will the musk carnations break and swell,
Soon shall we have gold-dusted snapdragon,
Sweet William with his homely cottage-smell,
And stocks in fragrant blow;
Roses that down the alley shine afar,
And open, jasmine-muffled lattices,
And groups under the dreaming garden trees,
And the full moon, and the white evening star.

   Matthew Arnold, 'Early June', Thyrsis, nineteenth
    century

Gather ye Rosebuds while ye may,
Old Time is still a-flying:
And this same flower that smiles to-day
To-morrow will be dying.

   Robert Herrick, 'To the Virgins, to Make Much of
    Time', seventeenth century

But pleasures are like poppies spread,
You seize the flower, its bloom is shed.

⇘ *Robert Burns*, 'Tam O'Shanter', *1790*

One of those old-fashioned paradises which
hardly exist any longer except as memories of
our childhood: no finical separation between
flower and kitchen garden there; no monotony of
enjoyment for one sense to the exclusion of
another but a charming paradisiacal mingling
of all that was pleasant to the eye and good for
food. The rich flower border running along every
walk, with its endless succession of spring flowers,
anemones, auriculas, wall flowers, sweet williams,
campanulas, snapdragons and tiger lilies had its
taller beauties such as moss and Provence roses,
varied with espalier apple trees; the crimson of a
carnation was carried out in the crimson of the
neighbouring strawberry beds; you gathered
a moss rose one moment and a bunch of currants
the next; you were in a delicious fluctuation

between the scent of jasmine and the juice of gooseberries.

↪ *George Eliot*, Scenes of Clerical Life, *1858*

Perfect moments come in every garden, though more frequently in some than others. To the very active gardener they may not be of great importance and usually they will be happy accidents, lucky moments when, chancing to glance up, the gardener will see that this or that grouping of plants at the height of their flowering looks exactly right, because of the way the light falls on them . . . The more contemplative gardener, seeing the garden as a whole, the design of it, and its nature as a still place of delight and refreshment, will wait and hope for the moment when it seems to achieve perfection . . .

But if they [the moments of perfection] may be planned and looked for, they cannot be preserved. Time will not stand still: we cannot freeze the perfect moment, we may only wait patiently for it to be repeated, and the very intensity of the pleasure such moments give comes precisely because of their transience and fragility – time is of their very essence. If a garden could be preserved at a moment of perfection and therefore set outside of time, it would become an embalmed garden, lifeless, and pointless as silk flowers.

✎ *Susan Hill and Rory Stuart*, Reflections from a
  Garden, *1995*

I know nothing so pleasant as to sit [in my garden] on a summer afternoon, with the western sun flickering through the great elder-trees, and lighting up our gay parterres, where flowers and flowering shrubs are set as thick as grass in a field, a wilderness of blossom, interwoven, intertwined, wreathy, garlandy, profuse beyond all profusion, where we may guess that there is such a thing as mould, but never see it. I know nothing so pleasant as to sit in the shade of that dark bower, with the eye resting on that bright piece of colour, lighted so gloriously by the evening sun, now catching a glimpse of the little birds as they fly rapidly in and

out of their nests – for there are always two or three
birds-nests in the thick tapestry of cherry-trees,
honeysuckles, and China-roses, which cover our
walls – now tracing the gay gambols of the common
butterflies as they sport around the dahlias; now
watching that rarer moth . . . the bird-bee, that
bird-like insect, which flutters in the hottest days
over the sweetest flowers, inserting its long
proboscis into the small tube of the jessamine, and
hovering over the scarlet blossoms of the geranium,
whose bright colour seems reflected on its own
feathery breast; that insect which seems so
thoroughly a creature of the air, never at rest;
always, even when feeding, self-poised and self-
supported, and whose wings, in their careless
motion, have a sound so deep, so full, so lulling, so
musical. Nothing so pleasant as to sit amid the
mixture of the flower and the leaf, watching the
bee-bird! Nothing so pretty to look at as my
garden! It is quite a picture; only unluckily it
resembles a picture in more qualities than one, – it
is fit for nothing but to look at. One might as well
think of walking in a framed canvass. There are

walks to be sure — tiny paths of smooth gravel, by
courtesy called such — but they are so overhung by
roses and lilies, and such gay encroachers — so
over-run by convolvulus, and heart's ease, and
mignonette, and other sweet stragglers, that, except
to edge through them occasionally, for the purposes
of planting, or weeding, or watering, there might as
well be no paths at all.

> ~ *Mary Russell Mitford*, 'Whitsun-Eve', Our Village,
>   *1820*

I was utterly alone with the sun and the earth. Lying
down on the grass, I spoke in my soul to the earth,
the sun, the air and the distant sea far beyond sight.
I thought of the earth's firmness — I felt it bear me
up; through the grassy couch there came an
influence as if I could feel the great earth speaking
to me. I thought of the wandering air — its pureness,
which is its beauty; the air touched me and gave me
something of itself . . . Then I addressed the
sun . . . I turned to the blue heaven over, gazing
into its depth, inhaling its exquisite colours and

sweetness. The rich blue of the unattainable flower of the sky drew my soul towards it, and there it rested, for pure colour is rest of heart. By all these I prayed; I felt an emotion of the soul beyond all definition . . . Then, returning, I prayed by the sweet thyme, whose little flowers I touched with my hand; by the slender grass; by the crumble of dry chalky earth I took up and let fall through my fingers. Touching the crumble of earth, the blade of grass, the thyme flower, breathing the earth-encircling air, thinking of the sea and the sky, holding out my hand for the sunbeams to touch it, prone on the sward in token of deep reverence . . . the inexpressible beauty of all filled me with a rapture, an ecstasy . . .

~ *Richard Jefferies*, The Story of My Heart, nineteenth century

I have often thought what a beautiful bit of summer gardening one could do, mainly planted with things usually grown in the kitchen garden only, and filling up spaces with quickly-grown flowering

118

plants. For climbers, there would be the Gourds
and marrows and Runner Beans; for splendour of
port and beauty of foliage, Globe Artichokes and
Sea-Kale, one of the grandest of blue-leaved plants.
Horse-radish also makes handsome tufts of its
vigorous deep-green leaves, and Rhubarb is one of
the grandest of large-leaved plants. Or if the garden
were in shape a double square, the further portion
being given to vegetables, why not have a bold
planting of these grand things as a division between
the two, and behind them a nine-feet high foliage-
screen of Jerusalem Artichoke? This Artichoke,
closely allied to our perennial Sunflowers, is also a
capital thing for a partition screen; a bed of it two or
three feet wide is a complete protection through the
summer and to the latest autumn.

∽ *Gertrude Jekyll*, Home and Garden, 1900

The pinks along my garden walks
Have all shot forth their summer stalks,
Thronging their buds 'mong tulips hot,
And blue forget-me-nots.

119

Their dazzling snows forth-bursting soon
Will lade the idle breath of June;
And waken thro' fragrant night
To steal the pale moonlight.

The nightingale at end of May
Lingers each year for their display;
Till when he sees their blossoms blown,
He knows that spring is flown.

June's birth, they greet, and when their bloom
Dislustres, withering on his tomb,
Then summer hath a shortening day;
And steps slow to decay.

꙰ *Robert Bridges*, 'Pinks', nineteenth century

An evening cloudburst
Sparrows cling desperately
To trembling bushes.

꙰ *Buson*, eighteenth century

And because the breath of flowers is far sweeter in the air (where it comes and goes like the warbling of music) than in the hand, therefore nothing is more fit for that delight, than to know what be the flowers and plants that do best perfume the air. Roses, damask and red, are fast flowers of their smells, so that you may walk by a whole row of them, and find nothing of their sweetness: yea, though it be in a morning dew. Bays likewise yield no smell as they grow, rosemary little, nor sweet-marjoram. That, which above all others, yields the sweetest smell in the air, is the violet, which comes twice a year, about the middle of April, and about Bartholomew-tide. Next to that is the musk rose, then the strawberry leaves dying with a most excellent cordial smell. Then the flower of the vines; it is a little dust . . . which grows upon the cluster in the first coming forth. Then sweet-briar, then wall-flowers, which are very delightful to be set under a parlour, or lower chamber window. Then pinks and gilliflowers, especially the matted pink, and clove gilliflower. Then the flowers of the lime-tree. Then the honeysuckles . . . But those which perfume the air most delightfully, not passed by as the rest, but being trodden upon and crushed, are three: that is burnet, wild-thyme and watermints. Therefore you are to set whole alleys of them, to have the pleasure when you walk or tread.

☞ *Sir Francis Bacon*, 'Of Gardens', *1625*

Fragrance in flower may, indeed, be described as their music, and it is none the less beautiful because it is silent. In every scented flower and leaf the perfume is exhaled by substances so perfectly blended that they give the impression of a single scent, just as several notes make a chord. We are all familiar with the dual sensation produced by smelling any sweet-scented flower – both an appreciation of the perfume and the still deeper pleasure afforded by something so delicately balanced and, as it were, faultlessly rounded that it seems almost beyond our mere human senses to enjoy it fully.

☞ *Eleanor Sinclair Rohde*, The Scented Garden, *1931*

We had a small garden beside our house; it was a fairyland to me, where miracles of beauty were of everyday occurrence. Every morning at an early hour I would run out from my bed to greet the first pink flush of dawn through the trembling leaves of the coconut trees which stood in a line along the garden boundary. The dewdrops glistened as the grass caught the first tremor of the morning breeze. The sky seemed to bring a personal companionship, and my whole body drank in the light and the peace of those silent hours. I was anxious never to miss a single morning because each one was more precious to me than gold to the miser. I had been blessed with that sense of wonder which gives a child his right to enter the treasure-house of mystery in the heart of existence.

Rabindranath Tagore, twentieth century

And truly, I reiterate . . . nothing's small!
No lily muffled hum of a summer bee
But finds some coupling with the spinning stars;
No pebble at your foot, but proves a sphere;

No chaffinch, but implies the cherubim
. . . Earth's crammed with heaven,
And every common bush afire with God:
But only he who sees, takes off his shoes.

     Elizabeth Barrett Browning, Aurora Leigh, Book VII,
     1857

If you take a flower in your hand and really look at
it, it's your world for the moment.

     Georgia O'Keefe, twentieth century

It began in dark and underground weather, a slow
hunger moving towards light . . . I saw it first in
early summer. It was a green and sleeping bud.
Ants worked around the unopened bloom,
gathering aphids and sap. A few days later, it was a
tender young flower, soft and new, with a pale green
center and a troop of silver gray insects climbing up
and down the stalk.

    Over the summer this sunflower grew into a
plant of incredible beauty, turning its face daily

toward the sun in the most subtle of ways, the black center of it dark and alive with a deep blue light, as if flint had sparked an elemental fire there, in community with rain, mineral, mountain air and sand.

As summer changed from green to yellow there were new visitors daily: the lace-winged insects, the bees whose legs were fat with pollen, and grasshoppers with their clattering wings and desperate hunger. There were other lives I missed, lives too small or hidden to see. It was as if this plant with its host of lives was a society, one in which moment by moment, depending on light and moisture, there was great and diverse change …

In this one plant, in one summer season, a drama of need and survival took place.

᠂ *Linda Hogan*, twentieth century

I've watched you now a full half-hour,
Self-poised upon that yellow flower;
And little Butterfly! Indeed
I know not if you sleep or feed.

How motionless! – not frozen seas
More motionless! And then
What joy awaits you, when the breeze
Hath found you out among the trees,
And calls you forth again!
This plot of orchard ground is ours;
My trees they are, my Sister's flowers;
Here rest your wings when they are weary;
Here lodge as in a sanctuary!
Come often to us, fear no wrong;
Sit near us on the bough!
We'll talk of sunshine and of song,
And summer days, when we were young;
Sweet childish days, that were as long
As twenty days are now.

   William Wordsworth, 'To a Butterfly', eighteenth
    century

These roses under my window make no reference
to former roses or to better ones; they are for what
they are; they exist with God to-day. There is no
time to them. There is simply the rose; it is perfect

in every moment of its existence. Before a leaf-bud has burst, its whole life acts; in the full-blown flower there is no more; in the leafless root there is no less. Its nature is satisfied, and it satisfies nature, in all moments alike. There is no time to it. But man postpones or remembers; he does not live in the present, but with reverted eye laments the past, or, heedless of the riches that surround him, stands on tiptoe to forsee the future. He cannot be happy and strong until he too lives with nature in the present, above time.

Ralph Waldo Emerson, Self-Reliance, *1841*

'Men', said the Little Prince, 'set out on their way in express trains, but they do not know what they are looking for. Then they rush about, and get excited, and turn round and round. And,' he added, 'it's not worth the trouble . . . what they are looking for could be found in a single rose . . .'

Antoine de Saint-Exupery, The Little Prince, *1943*

June is the month that takes care of itself. Even the dullest garden can't help being colourful in June. When the cow parsley reaches shoulder level in the hedgerows and the roadside is scented with honeysuckle and wild roses the garden too seems to grow up overnight. This is the time when one discovers if one has planted too closely, and I always have, and if one has staked sufficiently and efficiently, and I never have.

June is the month when roses tumble over the walls, the tall spikes of delphiniums tower above the jungle of the borders, at the mercy of the gales that nearly always turn up in June, to humble our pride and challenge our foresight.

   🙿 *Marjorie Fish*, A Flower for Every Day, *1965*

The moonbeam fell upon the roof and garden . . . It suffused the cottage with its brilliant light, except where the dark depth of the embowered porch defied its entry. All around the beds of flowers and herbs spread sparkling and defined. You could trace the minutest walk; almost distinguish every leaf. Now and then there came a breath, and the sweet-peas murmured in their sleep; or the roses rustled, as if they were afraid they were about to be roused from their lightsome dreams. Farther on the fruit trees caught the splendour of the night; and looked like a troop of sultanas taking their garden air, when the eye of man could not profane them, and laden with jewels. There were apples that rivalled rubies; pears of topaz tint; a whole paraphernalia of plums, some purple as amethyst, others blue and brilliant as the sapphire; and emerald here, and now a golden drop that gleamed like the yellow diamond of Gengis Khan.

Benjamin Disraeli, Sybil, chapter 5, *1845*

In Xanadu did Kubla Khan a stately pleasure-dome decree:
Where Alph, the sacred river, ran
Through caverns measureless to man.
Down to a sunless sea.
So twice five miles of fertile ground
With walls and towers were girdled round:

And there were gardens bright with sinuous rills,
And blossomed many an incense-bearing tree;
And here were forests ancient as the hills,
Enfolding sunny spots of greenery.

Samuel Taylor Coleridge, 'Kubla Khan', *1798*

Autumn

Without warning there's a sudden chill in the evening air as September arrives, announcing the imminence of autumn. Shadows lengthen and the days grow shorter. Still, the late-blooming flowers like asters, sedums, nerines, rudbeckias and chrysanthemums continue to cheer us, and dahlias will last until the first frosts. On a cloudless sunny day, with so much vibrant colour, you could almost believe it was still summer.

Autumn is the season of ripening – fruit reaches maturity, and seed forms. It's a time of abundance, with blackberries, raspberries, greengages, plums, damsons, quinces, pears and apples. Now we can gather the harvest and store fruit and vegetables, in one form or another – freezing, or making jams and chutneys. But as well as reaping the rewards of our labours, it's also a time for thanksgiving and sharing the bounty. Truly we can appreciate autumn's lesson that everything happens in its own good time – after the long seasons of preparation, planting and blossoming, we are richly rewarded by nature.

There's a mellowness about autumn, a softening of the light, a lessening of the tasks that have to be done in the garden, and a sense of completion. Leaves turn gold, russet and crimson. Vegetation begins to die down. Everything reaches its natural end, but we know it dies only to be re-born next spring. On warmer days spring bulbs can be planted, and we happily have a premonition of spring's certain return when we see the autumn crocuses and cyclamens.

As the leaves begin to fall and die, so too do we have an opportunity to reflect on, and let go of, all that no longer works in our own lives. As we set about clearing and putting the garden to bed for winter, or merely gaze upon the dying vegetation that was so fresh and colourful in spring and summer, we are reminded of how everything comes to an end when it has run its course. But nothing need ever be wasted. Whether it's consigning dead matter and fallen fruit to the compost heap, or brambles and roots of perennial weeds to the bonfire, or whether experiences and memories are transmuted into the rich matter of wisdom, new life can be born out of old. Composting gives the gardener the opportunity to experience first-hand the cycle of life, decay and renewal, and to co-operate with nature in making the soil productive. And for ourselves, we can take heart from this natural cycle, knowing that we are enriching our lives, just as the soil is enriched.

By late November most of the leaves have fallen, at first dry and crackly, then after autumn's necessary but depressing rains, wet and soggy. As we rake up the leaves for mulch, there is something reassuring in the knowledge that when decomposed, they too will improve the texture of the soil, or if we leave them on the flowerbeds they will provide protection from frost, and food for the myriad forms of life in the soil during the winter months.

Late autumn is also the time for digging and preparing new beds, and that most essential of tasks, spreading well-rotted manure on the surface, in readiness for the frost to do its beneficial winter work. But gradually, autumn gives way to winter, and it's time to retreat indoors to the fireside.

All things change, nothing is extinguished . . .
There is nothing in the whole world which is
permanent. Everything flows onward; all things are
brought into being with a changing nature . . .

    Ovid, Metamorphosis, first century

For everything there is a season, and a time for
every purpose under the heaven:

A time to be born, and a time to die;

A time to plant, and a time to pluck up that which is
planted . . .

    Ecclesiastes 3:1–2

It is He who sendeth the winds like heralds of glad
tidings going before his Mercy. When they have
carried the heavy-laden clouds, He drives them to a

land that is dead, makes rain to descend thereon,
and produces every kind of harvest . . .

≈ *The Koran*, Sura 7

With gentle flaws the western breeze
Into the garden saileth,
Scarce here and there stirring the single trees,
For his sharpness he vaileth;
So long a comrade of the bearded corn,
Now from the stubbles whence the shocks are borne,
O'er dewy lawns he turns to stray,
As mindful of the kisses and soft play
Wherewith he enamoured the light-hearted May,
Ere he deserted her;
Lover of fragrance, and too late repents;
Nor more of heavy hyacinth now may drink,
Nor spicy pink,
Nor summer's rose, nor garnered lavender,
But the few lingering scents
Of streaked pea, and gillyflower, and stocks
Of courtly purple, and aromatic phlox.

≈ *Robert Bridges*, 'The Garden in September', *1893*

For thou shalt eat the labour of thine hands; happy shalt thou be, and it shall be well with thee.

Thy wife shall be as a fruitful vine by the side of thine house; thy children like olive plants round about thy table.

❧ *Psalm 128:2–3*

Season of mists and mellow fruitfulness,
Close bosom-friend of the maturing sun;
Conspiring with him how to load and bless
With fruit the vines that round the thatch-eaves run;
To bend with apples the mossed cottage-trees,
And fill all fruit with ripeness to the core . . .

❧ *John Keats*, 'To Autumn', *1819*

Great is a ripe sunflower, and great was the sun above my corn-fields. His fingers lifted up the corn-ears, His hands fashioned my melons, and set my beans full in the pods. Therefore my heart is happy, and I will lay many blue prayer sticks at the shrine of Ta-Wa [the Creator].

Traditional Pueblo women's harvest song

What wond'rous Life is this I lead!
Ripe Apples drop about my head;
The Luscious Clusters of the Vine
Upon my Mouth do crush their Wine;
The Nectarene and curious Peach
Into my hands themselves do reach;
Stumbling on Melons, as I pass,
Insnar'd with Flow'rs, I fall on Grass . . .

Andrew Marvell, 'The Garden', c. 1651

We taste
Harvest: this instant
At the edge of green, on
The threshold of yellow,
Apple's perfection:
Taste frost, rain, sun,
White blaze of blossom

And celebration of the bees,
Taste labor of lady beetles
Keeping the tree clean.

Elsa Gidlow, twentieth century

The hot-headed man in the temple
Is like a tree grown in a garden;
Suddenly it bears fruit.
It reaches its end in the carpenting shop;
It is floated away far from its place,
Or fire is its funeral pyre.

The truly temperate man sets himself apart,
He is like a tree grown in a sunlit field,
But it flourishes, it doubles its yield,
It stands before its owner;
Its fruit is something sweet, its shade is pleasant.
And it reaches its end in a garden.

'Parable of Two Trees', The Instruction of
Amenemope, *c. 1100* BCE

My song is half a sigh
Because my green leaves die;
Sweet are my fruits, but all my leaves are dying;
And well may Autumn sigh,
And well may I
Who watch the sere leaves falling.
My leaves that fade and fall,
I note you one and all;
I call you, and the Autumn wind is calling,
Lamenting for your fall,
And for the pall
You spread on earth in falling.

ॐ *Christina Rossetti*, 'September', nineteenth century

The bad weather did not deter Katharine: the hour
had struck and the strategy of spring must be
worked out according to plan. This particular bulb
garden, with its many varieties of tulips, daffodils,
narcissi, hyacinths, and other spring blooms, was a
sort of double-duty affair. It must provide a bright
mass of color in May, and it must also serve as a
source of supply – flowers could be stolen from it

for the building of experimental centrepieces.

Armed with a diagram and a clipboard, Katharine . . . would sit, hour after hour, in the wind and the weather, while Henry Allen produced dozens of brown paper packages of new bulbs and a basketful of old ones, ready for the intricate internment. As the years went by and age overtook her, there was something comical yet touching in her bedraggled appearance on this awesome occasion – the small, hunched-over figure, her studied absorption in the implausible notion that there would be yet another spring, oblivious to the ending of her own days, which she knew perfectly well was near at hand, sitting there with her detailed chart under those dark skies in the dying October, calmly plotting the resurrection.

> *E. B. White*, in the introduction to his wife, Katharine S. White's book, Onward and Upward in the Garden, *1979*

Have you any flowers now? I have had a beautiful flower-garden this summer; but they are nearly gone now. It is very cold to-night, and I mean to pick the prettiest ones . . . and cheat Jack Frost of so many of the treasures he calculates to rob . . . Won't it be a capital idea to put him at defiance, for once at least, if no more? I would love to send you a bouquet . . . and you could press it and write under it, The last flowers of summer.

Emily Dickinson, letter to Abiah Root, *1845*

Why should this flower delay so long
To show its tremulous plumes?
Now is the time of plaintive robin-song,
When flowers are in their tombs.

Through the slow summer, when the sun
Called to each frond and whorl
That all he could for flowers was being done,
Why did it not uncurl?

It must have felt that fervid call
Although it took no heed,
Walking but now, when leaves like corpses fall,
And saps all retrocede.

Too late its beauty, lonely thing,
The season's shine is spent,
Nothing remains for it but shivering
In tempests turbulent.

Had it a reason for delay,
Dreaming in witlessness
That for a bloom so delicately gay
Winter would stay its stress?

— I talk as if the thing were born
With sense to work its mind;
Yet it is but one mask of many worn
By the Great Face behind.

   🙠 *Thomas Hardy*, 'The Last Chrysanthemum',
      nineteenth century

All that thy seasons bring, oh nature, is fruit for
me.
All things come from thee, subsist in thee, go back
to thee.

℞ *Marcus Aurelius*, Meditations, *180 AD*

You should see the joy with which I gaze on
manure heaps in which the eye of faith sees
Delaware grapes and D'Angoulême pears, and all
sorts of roses and posies.

℞ *Harriet Beecher Stowe*, nineteenth century

A good soil, like good food, must not be either too
fat, or heavy, or cold, or wet, or dry, or greasy, or
hard, or gritty, or raw; it ought to be like bread, like
gingerbread,, like a cake, like leavened dough; it
should crumble, but not break into lumps; under
the spade it ought to crack, but not squelch; it must
not make slabs, or blocks, or honeycombs, or
dumplings; but when you turn it over with a full
spade, it ought to breathe with pleasure and fall into

a fine and puffy tilth. That is a tasty and edible soil, cultured and noble, deep and moist, permeable, breathing and soft – in short, a good soil is like good people, and as is well-known there is nothing better in this vale of tears.

᷾ *Karel Čapek*, The Gardener's Year, *1929*

What I enjoy is not the fruits alone, but I also enjoy the soil itself, its nature and its power.

᷾ *Cicero*, first century BC

Treat the earth well. It was not given to you by your parents. It was lent to you by your children.

᷾ *Kenyan proverb*

Men seldom plant Trees till they begin to be Wise, that is, till they grow Old and find by Experience the Prudence and Necessity of it. When Ulysses, after a ten-years Absence, was return'd from Troy, and coming home, found his aged Father in the field planting of Trees, He asked him, why (being so far advanc'd in Years) he would put himself to the Fatigue and Labour of Planting that which he was never likely to enjoy the Fruits of? The good old Man (taking him for a Stranger) gently reply'd: I plant . . . against my Son Ulysses comes home.

☙ *John Evelyn*, seventeenth century

To have been placed on the earth 'to dress and keep it' was the divine intention; to make it a garden of delights for ourselves and our children, where the healthy prodding and stirring of the soil should produce, not only nourishing fruit for the body, but also most nourishable food for the mind.

☙ *St Augustine*, City of God, sixth century

The man who recognizes how he is linked with universal life is a man who possesses a sound soul because he is not isolated from his own energies, nor from the energies of nature. But as the highest form of life, man also becomes its guardian,

recognizing his very survival depends on seeing
that the fragile balance of nature, and living
organisms, is not disturbed.

✍ *Naveen Patnaik*, The Garden of Life, *1993*

There is not a flower that opens, not a seed that
falls into the ground, and not an ear of wheat that
nods on the end of its stalk in the wind that does
not preach and proclaim the greatness and mercy of
God to the whole world.

✍ *Thomas Merton*, The Seven Storey Mountain, *1948*

In my Autumn garden I was fain
To mourn among my scattered roses;
Alas for that last rosebud that uncloses
To Autumn's languid sun and rain
When all the world is on the wane!
Which has not felt the sweet constraint of June,
Nor heard the nightingale in tune.

Broad-faced asters by my garden walk,
You are but coarse compared with roses;
More choice, more dear that rosebud which
uncloses,
Faint-scented, pinched, upon its stalk,
That least and last which cold winds balk;
A rose it is though least and last of all,
A rose to me though at the fall.

᠅ *Christina Rossetti*, 'An October Garden', *1878*

I used to be ashamed of how much waste there was
even in my unpretentious garden here. I blamed
inexperience, impatience and extravagance. But
now I have come to accept that one must not count
the losses, they would be too alarming. One must
count only the joys, and feel continually blessed in
them. There is no unlucky gardener, for each small
success outweighs each defeat in his or her
passionate heart.

᠅ *May Sarton*, Plant Dreaming Deep, *1968*

You must not . . . be surprised if you have
moments in your gardening life of such profound
depression and disappointment that you will almost
wish you had been content to leave everything alone
and have no garden at all.

🌿 *Mrs C. W. Earle*, Pot-Pourri from a Surrey Garden,
1897

God grant me the serenity to accept the things I
cannot change, courage to change the things I can,
and wisdom to know the difference.

🌿 *Karl Reinhold Niebuhr*, 'The Serenity Prayer',
twentieth century

When I planted my pain in the field of patience it
bore fruit of happiness.

🌿 *Kahlil Gibran*, Spiritual Sayings of Kahlil Gibran,
1962

All flesh is grass, and all its beauty is like the flower of the field;

The grass withers, the flower fades, when the breath of the Lord blows upon it; surely the people is grass.

The grass withers, the flower fades; but the word of God will stand forever.

✍ *Isaiah 40:6–8*

It is easy for me to link salvation and compost. Compost has an almost mystical quality. It is made up of anything that is or was alive and is biodegradable – straw, spoiled hay, grass clippings, animal remains, manure, garbage, flesh, table scraps etc. A compost heap represents immortality. Nothing dies as such. All living things complete their cycle and return to the pool of life. There is neither beginning nor end, only the inexorable turning of the great wheel: growth, decay, death and rebirth.

✍ *William Frank Longgood*, Voices from the Earth: A Year in the Life of a Garden, *1991*

A few handfuls [of top-dressing] are easy to
scatter, and supply a true, slow-acting food rather
than a stimulant. Violent stimulants are apt to be
dangerous, promoting a soft, quick growth when
what the plant needs is a building-up of its
underground constitution, to take effect not
immediately and dramatically, but in months to
come.

The principle is always the same: you cannot
expect your soil and your plants to go on giving you
of their best if you are not prepared to give
something back in return. This is as true of gardens
as of human relationships.

~ *Vita Sackville-West*, Vita Sackville-West's Garden
    Book, *1968*

Now is the time for the burning of the leaves.
They go to the fire; the nostril pricks with smoke
Wandering slowly into a weeping mist.
Brittle and blotched, ragged and rotten sheaves!
A flame seizes the smouldering ruin and bites
On stubborn stalks that crackle as they resist.

The last hollyhock's fallen tower is dust;
All the spices of June are a bitter reek,
All the extravagant riches spent and mean.
All burns! The reddest rose is a ghost;
Sparks whirl up, to expire in the mist: the wild
Fingers of fire are making corruption clean.

Now is the time for stripping the spirit bare,
Time for the burning of days ended and done,
Idle solace of things that have gone before:
Rootless hopes and fruitless desire are there;
Let them go to the fire, with never a look behind.
The world that was ours is a world that is ours no
     more.

They will come again, the leaf and the flower, to arise
From squalor of rottenness into the old splendour,
And magical scents to a wondering memory bring;
The same glory, to shine upon different eyes.
Earth cares for her own ruins, naught for ours.
Nothing is certain, only the certain spring.

   Laurence Binyon, 'The Burning of the Leaves', *1944*

The good gardener knows with absolute certainty that if he does his part, if he gives the labour, the love, and every aid that his knowledge of his craft, experience of the conditions of his place, and exercise of his personal wit can work together to suggest, that so surely will God give the increase. Then with the honestly-earned success comes the consciousness of encouragement to renewed effort, and, as it were, an echo of the gracious words, 'Well done, good and faithful servant.'

Gertrude Jekyll, Wood and Garden, *1899*

To you the earth yields her fruit, and you shall not want if you but know how to fill your hands.

It is in exchanging the gifts of the earth that you shall find abundance and be satisfied . . .

Kahlil Gibran, The Prophet, *1923*

. . . What pleasure is there greater than to go round one's garden on a sunny day with a fellow enthusiast, and to sing that cheering Litany which runs . . . 'Oh, wouldn't you like a bit of this?' – 'And I could send you a bulb of that.' Down delves the glad trowel into a clump, and it is halved – like mercy, blessing him that gives and him that takes.

 ✺ *R. J. Farrer*, In a Yorkshire Garden, *1909*

God made a little gentian;
It tried to be a rose
And failed, and all the summer laughed.
But just before the snows
There came a purple creature
That ravished all the hill;
And summer hid her forehead,
And mockery was still.
The frosts were her condition;
The Tyrian would not come
Until the North evoked it.
'Creator! Shall I bloom?'

 ✺ *Emily Dickinson*, Collected Poems of Emily Dickinson, *1924*

Nature's peace will flow into you as sunshine flows into trees. The winds will blow their own freshness into you, and the storms their energy, while cares will drop off like autumn leaves.

᷍ *John Muir*, nineteenth century

A person becomes a flowering orchard. The person that does good work is indeed this orchard bearing good fruit.

᷍ *Hildegard of Bingen*, twelfth century

There is something more at stake here than simply trying to justify why a gardener might wish to talk to plants. Traditional peoples around the world have always asserted that the process of food gathering is an act of gift giving from prey to person. It is said that the spirit of the gift increases even as the body of the gift is consumed. The predator who forgets to acknowledge the gift suffers dire consequences.

᷍ *Jim Nollman*, Why We Garden: Cultivating a Sense of Place, *1994*

Here I am again with my sickle, spade, hoe
To decide over life and death, presume to call
This plant a 'weed', that one a 'flower',
Adam's prerogative, hereditary power
I can't renounce. And yet I know, I know,
It is a single generator drives them all,
And drives my murderous, my ordering hand.

These foxgloves, these red poppies, I let them
    stand,
Though I did not sow them. Slash the fruit-bearing
    bramble,
Dig out ground elder, bindweed, stinging nettle,
Real rivals, invaders, whose roots ramble,
Robbing or strangling those of more delicate
    plants.
Or perhaps it's their strength, putting me on my
    mettle
To fight them for space, resist their advance.
I stop. I drop the spade,
Mop my face, consider;
Who's overrun the earth
And almost outrun it?

Who'll make it run out?
Who bores and guts it,
Pollutes and mutates it,
Corrodes and explodes it?
Each leaf that is laid
On the soil will feed it,
Turning death into birth.
If the cycle is breaking
Who brought it about?

I shall go again to the overgrown plot
With my sickle, hoe, spade,
But use no weedkiller, however selective,
No chemicals, no machine.
Already the nettles, ground elder, bindweed
Spring up again.
It's a good fight, as long as neither wins,
There are fruit to pick, unpoisoned,
Weeds to look at. I call them 'wildflowers'.

ఞ *Michael Hamburger*, 'Weeding', *1977*

Trench deep; dig in the rotting weeds;
Slash down the thistle's greybeard seeds;
Then make the frost your servant; make
His million fingers pry and break
The clods by glittering midnight stealth
Into the necessary tilth.

Vita Sackville-West, 'Autumn', The Land, *1926*

All my hurts my garden spade can heal.

Ralph Waldo Emerson, Musketaquid, *1847*

For I do believe that the Blessing of God is much
Assisting to those who Love and endeavour to
Improve and Preserve his Works; for God's Works
and his Word are no such different things;
Therefore you that are lovers of trees and plants, if
once you have them, let your Love be shewed in the
care you take of them.

Moses Cook, The Manner of Raising Ordering and
    Improving Forest and Fruit Trees, *1679*

[In the garden] the door is always open into the
'holy' – growth, birth, death. Every flower holds the
whole mystery in its short cycle, and in the garden
we are never far away from death, the fertilizing
good, creative death.

  🙠 *May Sarton*, Journal of a Solitude, *1973*

God of gardeners, accept this coil
Of acrid smoke from nettle and weed,
This left-hand mound of sinful soil
That I have sifted from the seed.

With hoe and mattock, spade and rake,
From morning dew to evening grace,
My back has bended for Thy sake,
To bring sweet order to this place.

Thy fruits and tubers basketed,
Thy flowers lit from setting sun,
With fragrant heart and reverent head
I tend this altar gleaming red,
As my forefathers must have done.

  🙠 *Richard Church*, 'Twelve Noon', *1936*

What is born will die,
What has been gathered will be dispersed,
What has been accumulated will be exhausted,
What has been built up will collapse . . .

✍ *The Buddha*, sixth century BC

Close to the gates a spacious Garden lies,
From storms defended, and inclement skies:
Four acres was th' allotted space of ground,
Fenc'd with a green enclosure all around.
Tall thriving trees confess'd the fruitful mold;
The red'ning apple ripens here to gold,
Here the blue fig with luscious juice o'erflows,
With deeper red the full pomegranate glows,
The branch here bends the weighty pear,
And verdant olives flourish round the year,
The balmy spirit of the western gale
Eternal breathes on fruits untaught to fail:
Each dropping pear a following pear supplies,
On apples apples, figs on figs arise:
The same mild season gives the blooms to blow
The buds to harden, and the fruits to grow.

Here order's vines in equal ranks appear,
With all th' united labours of the year;
Some to unload the fertile branches run,
Some day the black'ning clusters in the sun,
Others to tread the liquid harvest join,
The groaning presses foam with floods of wine.
Here are the vines in early flow'r descry'd,
Here grapes discoloured on the sunny side,
And there in autumn's richest purple dy'd.
Beds of all various herbs, for ever green,
In beauteous order terminate the scene.

≈ *Homer*, 'The Garden of Alcinous', The Odyssey,
   eighth century BC, translated by Alexander Pope,
   1725

In my compost pile . . . the leaves are all different
kinds. There are grass clippings too, weeds, small
twigs, and kitchen leavings. As I turn the pile over,
everything joins with everything else. It is hard to
know any longer what is what because it is mixed
together, on the way to becoming one thing, soil. I
take comfort in this. Through the seasons my

memories are composted too, and like the leaves they come together. Turned over and over, in time they finally turn into something new – rich, dark earth in the palm of my hand.

Gunilla Norris, Journeying in Place: Reflections from a Country Garden, *1994*

The painted autumn overwhelms
The summer's routed last array
The citron patches on the elms
Bring sunshine to a sunless day.

The dahlias and chrysanthemums
Droop in the dripping garden lane,
A drowsy insect hums and drums
Across the imprisoning window-pane.

The creeper's hatchment red and brown
Falls gently on the garden bed.
The lurid snow-cloud on the down
Can scarcely hide the winter's head.

John Meade Falkner, 'Epilogue', *1933*

The soul in the body is like sap in a tree, and the soul's powers are like the form of the tree. How? The intellect in the soul is like the greenery of the tree's branches and leaves, the will like its flowers, the mind like its bursting first fruits, the reason like the perfected mature fruit, and the senses like its size and shape. And so a person's body is strengthened and sustained by the soul. Hence, O human, understand that you are in your soul . . .

Hildegard of Bingen, Scivias (Scrito vias Domine or Know the Ways of the Lord), Book I, *1165*

Winter

Rest and renewal are winter's themes, and time for taking stock and planning for the future. With the late jobs of clearing and tidying the garden completed, the ground is now too hard for digging and too cold for planting. Fog and damp make the garden uninviting, and on days when the frost lingers because of low daytime temperatures, there's no better place to be than indoors.

We don't have to work in the garden because the plants are asleep, though on those occasional days when milder temperatures enable us to be outside, the fresh air and winter's unique beauty energise us, and inspire us to make plans for the coming year's new cycle of growth. This respite from work in the garden can be a creative time. It's a time of reflection, of examining our successes and failures, and of aspiring to achieve an even more rewarding collaboration with nature. Slowly, over time, with patience and experience, we acquire knowledge, we experiment, keep records and borrow ideas, and winter enables us to review all this. We can allow our imagination free rein as we sit by the fire reading our gardening books, armchair-travelling to foreign gardens, revelling in seed and plant catalogues, and dreaming our gardens into existence. Imagination and dreams are vital, for without them we create nothing.

The garden may be asleep, but it is far from dead, whatever it may look like. Life is merely pausing and waiting to bloom. Beneath the soil spring bulbs are actively growing, and worms are hard at work, along with millions of micro-organisms, helping to keep the soil healthy and productive for the future. Similarly, in our personal lives, even though there are empty and dark periods when nothing appears to be happening, beneath the surface there is activity and shifts are taking place as a prelude to change. Growth is happening, and acceptance and trust that all shall be well are important at such times.

Cold and darkness are a necessary part of nature's cycle, but on a milder day when the sun breaks through, there are still some tasks that can be done outside, like the winter pruning and thinning out of fruit trees, checking on plants that need protection, tying in climbers that have been loosened by the wind, or making sure alpines are not covered with leaves. It's better to leave tops and seed-heads on plants, however, until the spring, because they offer some protection and provide food for birds. They can also look splendid in winter conditions. Nothing is more exquisite in winter than the filigree tracery of frosting or a sprinkling of snow on trees and shrubs, particularly at the time of the winter solstice when the red berries of holly provide a dramatic contrast.

But at the turn of the year it can be a difficult time for birds and animals, as well as humans. Biting winds prevail; snow melts only to freeze over again; and we're aware of the silence, with birds in their nests or far away in warmer climes. Winter can seem to go on forever, but hope sustains us. Even in the bleakest and coldest of times there are signs of life which bolster our faith in what lies ahead. It's life-affirming to wander in the garden and see the signs of regeneration to come. We can appreciate the bright red, orange and yellow dogwood stems or the corkscrew willow whose contorted form suddenly surprises us with catkins. There's also the flowering winter honeysuckle, and the sarcoccas with their fabulous winter fragrance, and likewise wintersweet, mahonia and viburnum to delight us.

The last days of winter can be almost spring-like. In spite of wind and rain, and the occasional snowfall or hailstorm, a day or two of blue skies and sunshine are so welcome and presage what is to come. Before long the first snowdrops, the harbingers of spring, thrust their way through mud, dead leaves and moss immaculately white with their pretty green markings, and the hellebores stand erect with flowers of maroon, pink, ivory and softest lime.

There are signs of life all around us and it's a joy to see what has survived the winter. Gradually the light increases and the days become slightly warmer. We can cut back last year's blackened growth and add to the compost heap; we can start to sow seed indoors; and the next phase of our stewardship can begin, just as the crocuses burst through the soil – and we know that spring is imminent.

Love winter when the plant says nothing.

  Thomas Merton, twentieth century

The world's a garden; pleasures are the flowers,
Of fairest hues, in form and number many:
The lily, first, pure whitest flower of any,
Rose sweetest rare, with pinked gillyflowers,
The violet, and double marigold,
And pansy too: but after all mischances,
Death's winter comes and kills with sudden cold
Rose, lily, violet, marigold, pink, pansies.

  William Shakespeare, 'The Garden', *1621*

Ah Sun-flower! weary of time,
Who countest the steps of the Sun:
Seeking after that sweet golden clime,
Where the traveller's journey is done.

Where the youth pined away with desire,
And the pale Virgin shrouded in snow:
Arise from their graves and aspire,
Where my Sun-flower wishes to go.

✌ *William Blake*, 'Ah Sun-flower!', *1794*

God gave us memories that we might have roses in December.

✌ *J. M. Barrie*, Courage, *1922*

To garden, to garner up the seasons in a little space, is part of every wise man's philosophy. To sow the seeds, to watch the tender shoots come out and brave the light and rain, to see the buds lift up their heads, and then to catch one's breath as the flowers open and display their precious colours, living, breathing jewels, is enough to live for. But there is more than that. A man may choose the feast to spread before his eyes, may sow old memories and see them grow, and feel the answering colours in his heart. This Rose he used to pass on his way to school; it nodded to him over the high red wall, while next to it a Purple Clematis clung . . . This patch of Golden Marigolds reminds him of a long border in the garden where he spent his boyhood . . . Plant memories, indeed! A man may plant a host of them and never then recapture all his joys . . . There is something more than memory in a garden. There is that urgent need man has to be part of growing life . . . There is that in the hum and business of a garden that makes for peace; the senses are softly stirred even as the heart finds wings. No greeting is as sweet as the drowsy murmur of bees . . . No day so good as that which breaks to a song of birds. No sight so happy as the elegant confusion of flower-border still wet and glistening with morning dew.

✿ *Dion Clayton Calthrop*, The Charm of Gardens, *1910*

Gardeners, like everyone else, live second by second and minute by minute. What we see at one particular moment is then and there before us. But there is a second way of seeing. Seeing with the eye

of memory, not the eye of our anatomy, calls up
days and seasons past and years gone by.

☙ *Allen Lacey*, The Gardener's Eye, *1992*

When I was quite a boy my father used to take me
to the Montpelier Tea-Gardens at Walworth . . . I
unlock the casket of memory, and draw back the
warders of the brain; and there this scene of my
infant wanderings still lives unfaded, or with
fresher dyes. A new sense comes upon me, as in a
dream; a richer perfume, brighter colours start out;
my eyes dazzle; my heart heaves with its new load of
bliss, and I am a child again. My sensations are all
glossy, spruce, voluptuous and fine: they wear a
candied coat, and are in holiday trim. I see the beds
of larkspur with purple eyes; tall holyoaks, red and
yellow; the broad sunflowers, caked in gold, with
bees buzzing round them; wildernesses of pinks,
and hot-glowing peonies; poppies run to seed; the
sugared lily, and faint mignionette, all ranged in
order, and as thick as they can grow; the box-tree
borders; the gravel walks, the painted alcove, the

confectionery, the clotted cream: I think I see them now with sparkling looks; or have they vanished while I have been writing this description of them? No matter; they will return again when I least think of them. All that I have observed since, of flowers and plants, and grass-plots, and of suburb delights, seem to me borrowed from 'that first garden of my innocence' – to be slips and scions stolen from that bed of memory.

✌ *William Hazlitt*, Why Distant Objects Please, *1822*

Restfulness is the prevailing note of an old garden; in this fairy world of echo and suggestion where the Present never comes but to commune with the Past, we feel the glamour of a Golden Age, of a state of society just and secure which has grown and blossomed as the rose. How few there are who are incapable of feeling the mysterious appeal of such a place – of the scenes which reflect upon us the passion and happiness of bygone generations, the statues which gleam out under the deepening spell of the twilight like phantoms of old-world greatness, the still pools that slumber in the sunshine and call our spirits to their dreamland of abiding peace, the rippling music of the fountain, like trills of elfin laughter and the hoarse water-voices that are hasting with passionate earnestness to the everlasting sea. But beyond all there is a deeper mystery. In such scenes there is the same elusive suggestiveness that is found in the perfume of flowers. That which is interesting is real, and the old garden is very real. It has the power of fixing attention, it grips you by the sleeve, it is instinct with a silent eloquence; you feel in the Spiritualist phrase that it is 'seeking to communicate', to open vistas into the past, that it has a secret to unfold, a message to deliver. What then is the secret of the old-world garden? This, — that it knows us well. We have come back to an earlier home, to scenes which are strangely familiar to us, to the life of former generations whose being was one with ours. Every living creature is adapted to its environment by changes in brain structure produced either by the natural selection of accidental variations or by multitudinous repetition of the same impressions and the same actions. It is this harmony with the surroundings which we feel upon entering an old house or garden; vague ancestral memories are faintly stirred and the sentiment which may attach to objects that have been habitual sources of enjoyment to generation after generation.

☙ *Sir George Sitwell*, On the Making of Gardens, *1909*

A gardener is never shut out from his garden, wherever he may be. Its comfort never fails. Though the city may close about him, he can still wander in his garden, does he but close his eyes.

☙ *Beverley Nichols*, twentieth century

Nurturing, decisive, interfering, cajoling, gardeners are eternal optimists who trust the ways of nature and believe passionately in the idea of *improvement*. As the gnarled, twisted branches of apple trees have taught them, beauty can spring in the most unlikely places. Patience, hard work, and a clever plan usually lead to success; private worlds of color, scent, and astonishing beauty. Small wonder a gardener plans her garden as she wishes she could plan her life.

ல Diane Ackerman, Cultivating Delight: A Natural History of My Garden, 2001

Their gardeners are not only botanists, but also painters and philosophers, having a thorough knowledge of the human mind, and the arts by which its strongest feelings are excited … In China, gardening is a distinct profession, requiring an extensive study; to the perfect of which few arrive. The gardeners then, far from being either ignorant or illiterate, are men of high abilities . . . it is in consideration of these accomplishments only that they are permitted to exercise their profession, for with the Chinese the taste of ornamental gardening is an object of legislative attention, it being supposed to have an influence upon the general culture, and consequently upon the beauty of the whole country. They observe, that mistakes committed in this art, are too important to be tolerated, being much exposed to view, and in great measure irreparable; as it often requires the space of a century, to redress the blunders of an hour.

~ *Sir William Chambers*, A Dissertation on Oriental Gardening, *1772*

People who blame their failures on 'not having a green thumb' (and they are legion) usually haven't done their homework. There is of course no such thing as a green thumb. Gardening is a vocation like any other – a calling, if you like, but not a gift from heaven.

~ *Eleanor Perenyi*, Green Thoughts, *1981*

If you wish to make anything grow you must understand it, and understand it in a very real sense. 'Green fingers' are a fact, and a mystery only to the unpractised. But green fingers are the extensions of a verdant heart. A good garden cannot be made by somebody who has not developed the capacity to know and love growing things.

~ *Russell Page*, The Education of a Gardener, *1962*

Our way is to see what we are doing, moment after moment.

☙ *Shunryu Suzuki*, twentieth century

The old man stopped from his work, as the musing figure of his guest darkened the prospect before him, and said, –

'A pleasant time, sir for the gardener!'

'Ay, is it so? You must miss the fruits and flowers of summer.'

'Well, sir, – but we are now paying back the garden for the good things it has given us. It is like taking care of a friend in old age, who has been kind to us when he was young.' . . .

''Tis a winning thing, sir, a garden! It brings us an object every day; and that's what I think a man ought to have if he wishes to lead a happy life.'

☙ *Edward Bulwer-Lytton*, Eugene Aram, nineteenth century

It was the sweetest, most mysterious-looking place anyone could imagine. The high walls which shut it in were covered with the leafless stems of climbing roses, which were so thick that they were matted together. Mary Lennox knew they were roses because she had seen a great many roses in India . . . The sun was shining inside the four walls and the high arch of blue sky over this particular piece of Misselthwaite seemed even more brilliant and soft than it was over the moor. The robin flew down from his tree-top and hopped about or flew after her from one bush to another. He chirped a good deal and had a very busy air, as if he were showing her things. Everything was strange and silent, and she seemed to be hundreds of miles away from anyone, but somehow she did not feel lonely at all. All that troubled her was her wish that she knew whether all the roses were dead, or if perhaps some of them had lived and might put out leaves and buds as the weather got warmer. She did not want it to be a quite dead garden. If it were a quite alive garden, how wonderful it would be, and what thousands of roses would grow on every side?

🌸 *Frances Hodgson Burnett*, The Secret Garden, *1911*

To create a garden is to search for a better world. In our effort to improve on nature, we are guided by a vision of paradise. Whether the result is a horticultural masterpiece or only a modest vegetable patch, it is based on the expectation of a glorious future. This hope for the future is at the heart of all gardening.

🌸 *Marina Schinz*, Visions of Paradise: Themes and Variations on the Garden, *1989*

A garden is always a series of losses set against a few triumphs, like life itself.

🌸 *May Sarton*, At Seventy, *1984*

Everything is gestation and then bringing forth.

🌸 *Rainer Maria Rilke*, Letters to a Young Poet, *1903*

A garden is a grand teacher. It teaches patience and careful watchfulness; it teaches industry and thrift; above all it teaches entire trust.

∻ *Gertrude Jekyll*, Wood and Garden, *1899*

To accomplish great things, we must not only act, but also dream, not only plan, but also believe.

∻ *Anatole France*, twentieth century

How strange it is that no country name compares snowdrops with bells for they are bell-like as they swing to and fro. How do they swing on those delicate threads which connect flower to stem. You'd think they would be torn off. But they can stand any gale that blows. They yield to the wind rather than oppose it. A tree may be blown down in the night but never a single snowdrop head is blown off. Their strength is that they know when to give in.

∻ *H. L. V. Fletcher*, Popular Flowering Plants, *1971*

Do you know what I was, how I lived? You know
what despair is: then
winter should have meaning for you.
I did not expect to survive,
earth suppressing me, I didn't expect
to waken again, to feel
in damp earth my body
able to respond again, remembering
after so long how to open again
in the cold light
of earliest spring —
afraid, yes, but among you again
crying yes risk joy
in the raw wind of the new world.

∽ *Louise Gluck*, 'Snowdrops', *1992*

A garden is not made in a year; indeed it is never
made in the sense of finality. It grows, and with the
labour of love should go on growing.

∽ *Frederick Eden*, A Garden in Venice, *1903*

What more remains to say of the garden, now shorn of its beauty, except that each year one learns to love it more? Alone, defying frost and sleet, the tall blue monks-hood spire remains, to be stricken down in turn, and patiently awaits the dawn of spring.

❧ *George H. Ellwanger*, The Garden's Story, *1889*

In the depth of winter, I finally learned that within me there lay an invincible summer.

❧ *Albert Camus*, twentieth century

To a gardener, life after death is a bottomless mystery, but one he accepts pretty much as a certainty . . . so that snow comes as a promise of new life ahead. Snow covers the failures of the past, too. The weedy corners are obliterated, the rough brown lawn is smooth and clean. Last year is forgotten. We look ahead. Next year is going to be better. We start planning for a year like nothing we ever saw before.

❧ *Richard C. Davids*, Garden Wizardry, *1976*

. . . This passion for winter flowers has its roots deep, deep within me. I have a horror of endings, of farewells, of every sort of death. The inevitable curve of Nature, which rises so gallantly and falls so ignominiously, is to me a loathsome shape. I want the curve to rise perpetually. I want the rocket, which is life, to soar to measureless heights. I shudder at its fall . . . I believe that my love for winter flowers has its secret in this neurosis . . . I want my garden to *go on*. I cannot bear to think of it as a place that may be tenanted only in the easy months. I will not have it draped with Nature's dust sheets. That is why I wage this battle for winter flowers . . .

➚ *Beverly Nichols*, Down the Garden Path, *1932*

There is a wonderful beauty in the old stems . . . of many plants in a soft winter's evening glow. A ruddy light on brown Grasses or Eryngium stems, or against bare Lime twigs, is a source of great pleasure when it is just too dark to see to weed or dig . . . Then again on a frosty morning, every stem,

weed, blade of grass or cobweb has its edging of
pearls or diamond dust, and I am always glad if I
have not yet tidied away the dead stems that look so
lovely in their coats of hoar-frost.

᠁ *E. A. Bowles*, My Garden in Autumn and Winter,
1915

If there were no tribulation, there would be no rest;
if there were no winter, there would be no summer.

᠁ *St John Chrysostom*, fourth/fifth century

A garden is evidence of faith. It links us with all
the misty figures of the past who also planted and
were nourished by the fruits of their planting.

᠁ *Gladys Taber*, Stillmeadow Sampler, 1959

The enjoyments of a garden being so manifold and
continuous, bringing brightness to the home,
health to the body, and happiness to the mind, it is
for us, who have proved them, whose daily lives are

made more cheerful by their influence, out of gratitude and our goodwill, to invite and to instruct others that they may share our joy.

🙠 *S. Reynolds Hole*, Our Garden, nineteenth century

November smells of rue, bitter and musty,
Of mould, and fungus, and fog at the blue dusk.
The Church repents, and the trees, scattering their riches,
Stand up in bare bones.
But already the green buds sharpen for the first spring day,
Red embers glow on the twigs of pyrus japonica,
And clematis awns, those burnished curly wigs,
Feather for the seeds' flight.

Stark Advent songs, the busy fungus of decay —
They are works of darkness that prepare the light,
And soon the candid frost lays bare all secrets.

🙠 *Anne Ridler*, 'Winter Poem', The Collected Poems, *1994*

A Gard'ner's Work is never at an end; it begins with the Year, and continues to the next.

   John Evelyn, Kalendarium Hortense, *1664*

When the winter chrysanthemums go, there's nothing to write about but radishes.

   Matsuo Basho, seventeenth century

One grows restless to be growing things. Gardens promise reincarnation. A garden is nature in miniature, under one's guard and manipulation, if not complete control. Watching nature grow, one connects with one's own growth, not simply from point A to point B, but the way one grows into an activity or an idea. So like hibernating animals, gardeners wait in suspense for spring. Nature is beautiful in winter, and we *need* to find it so . . . In winter, enjoying the garden requires effort. I try to think of the beds as hibernating, not ruined, because I know they will return with gusto in a few months, and I don't want my senses to starve in the meantime.

�─ *Diane Ackerman*, Cultivating Delight: A Natural History of my Garden, *2001*

We never keep to the present. We recall the past; we anticipate the future as if we found it too slow coming and were trying to hurry it up, or we recall the past as if to stay its too rapid flight.

�─ *Blaise Pascal*, twentieth century

A garden may be a re-creation on earth of the mythical garden from which man came or an anticipation of an ideal other-world to which he may ultimately pass. The gardener looks back to Paradise, or looks forward to Heaven.

�─ *Miles and John Hadfield*, Gardens of Delight, *1964*

The art of gardening is evaluating what you have got and transforming it into what you want.

☙ *Nigel Colborn*, The Garden Sourcebook: The Essential Guide to Planting and Plants, *1993*

Gardens are refuges. In search of replenishment we retreat to them as to a safe haven. They have none of the threatening attributes to be found in more dramatic escapes: lone voyages, wilderness, deserts – or drugs. There is no need to pit your endurance against the elements, to feel challenged or to prove yourself to yourself. Gardens act as a solace and a panacea. With their innumerable qualities we use them in a variety of ways, for inspiration or freedom, for discovery or surrender.

☙ *Mirabel Osler*, A Breath from Elsewhere, *1997*

The many great gardens of the world, of literature and poetry, of painting and music, of religion and architecture, all make the point as clear as possible: the soul cannot thrive in the absence of a garden. If you don't want paradise, you are not human; and if you are not human, you don't have a soul.

❦ *Thomas Moore*, The Re-Enchantment of Everyday Life, *1996*

Cold is the winter day, misty and dark:
The sunless sky with faded gleams is rent:
And patches of thin snow outlying, mark
The landscape with a drear disfigurement.

The trees their mournful branches lift aloft:
The oak with knotty twigs is full of trust,
With bud-thonged bough the cherry in the croft;
The chestnut holds her gluey knops upthrust.

No birds sing, but the starling chaps his bill
And chatters mockingly; the newborn lambs

Within their strawbuilt fold beneath the hill
Answer with plaintive cry their bleating dams.

Their voices melt in welcome dreams of spring,
Green grass and leafy trees and sunny skies:
My fancy decks the woods, the thrushes sing,
Meadows are gay, bees hum and scents arise.

And God the Maker doth my heart grow bold
To praise for wintry works not understood,
Who all the worlds and ages doth behold,
Evil and good as one, and all as good.

  🌹 *Robert Bridges*, 'January', The Poetical Works of
     Robert Bridges, nineteenth century

For as the garden keeps changing, so does the
gardener . . . while the spirit is still soaring eagerly
onward and upward, the old bones and cartilage
begin to insist that they can no longer handle the
demands being made on them. This is obviously
unfair and a better system should be devised . . . In

the new system I would propose we should all go
vigorously full speed ahead until our time was up,
then fall suddenly on our faces, finished.
Montaigne, the essayist, said he hoped Death would
find him planting cabbages. I myself would like to
meet Death in the flower garden — falling face down
on to a cushion of *Dianthus gratianopolitanus*, if it's
not too much to ask.

🙠 *Elizabeth Sheldon*, Time and the Gardener, 2003

The Snowdrop, Winter's timid child,
Awakes to life, bedew'd with tears,
And flings around its fragrance mild;
And when no rival flowerets bloom,
Amidst the bare and chilling gloom,
A beauteous gem appears!

All weak and wan, with head inclin'd,
Its parent-breast the drifted snow,
It trembles, while the ruthless wind
Bends its slim form; the tempest lowers,
Its em'rald eye drops crystal show'rs
On its cold bed below.

Poor flow'r! On thee the sunny beam
No touch of genial warmth bestows!
Except to thaw the icy stream
Whose little current purls along,
And whelms thee as it flows.

Where'er I find thee, gentle flower,
Thou still art sweet, and dear to me!
For I have known the cheerless hour,
Have seen the sun-beams cold and pale,
Have felt the chilling, wintry gale,
And wept, and shrunk like thee!

☙ *Mary 'Perdita' Robinson*, 'Ode to the Snowdrop',
   eighteenth century

Take January's advice. Stack wood,
Weather inevitably turns cold, and you

Make fires to stay healthy. Study
The grand metaphor of this yearly work.

Wood is a symbol for absence. Fire,
For your love of God. We burn form

To warm the soul. Soul loves winter
For that, and accepts reluctantly the

Comfort of spring with its elegant,
Proliferating gifts. All part of the

Plan: fire becoming ash becoming
Garden soil becoming mint, willow, and tulip . . .

✆   *Rumi*, 'An Armor of roses' (thirteenth century),
    The Glance: Songs of Soul Meeting, translated by
    Coleman Barks, *1999*

The fair-weather-gardener, who will do nothing
except when wind and weather and everything else
are favourable, is never a master of his craft.
Gardening, above all crafts, is a matter of faith,
grounded, however . . . on his experience that
somehow or other seasons go on in their right
course, and bring their right results. No doubt bad

seasons are a trial of his faith; it is grievous to lose the fruits of much labour by a frosty winter or a droughty summer, but, after all, frost and drought are necessities for which, in all his calculations, he must leave an ample margin . . .

> *Canon Henry Ellacombe*, In a Gloucestershire Garden, *1895*

I never see a great garden . . . but I think of the calamities that have visited it, unsuspected by the delighted visitor who supposes it must be nice to garden here.

It is not nice to garden anywhere. Everywhere there are violent winds, startling once-per-five centuries floods, unprecedented droughts, record-setting freezes, abusive and blasting heats never known before. There is no place, no garden, where these terrible things do not drive gardeners mad …

There are no green thumbs or black thumbs. There are only gardeners and non-gardeners. Gardeners are the ones who ruin after ruin get on with the high defiance of nature herself, creating, in the very face of her chaos and tornado, the bower of roses and the pride of irises . . . Defiance . . . is what makes gardeners.

☙ *Henry Mitchell*, The Essential Earthman, *1981*

Let no one be discouraged by the thought of how much there is to learn . . . the first steps are steps into a delightful unknown, the first successes are victories all the happier for being scarcely expected, and with the growing knowledge comes the widening outlook, and the comforting sense of an ever-increasing gain of critical appreciation. Each new step becomes a little surer, and each new grasp a little firmer, till, little by little, comes the power of intelligent combination, the nearest thing we can know to the mighty force of creation.

☙ *Gertude Jekyll*, Wood and Garden, *1899*

Effort is its own reward.
We are here to do,
And through doing to learn;
And through learning to know;
And through knowing to experience wonder;
And through wonder to attain wisdom;
And through wisdom to find simplicity;
And through simplicity to give attention;
And through attention
To see what needs to be done . . .

   Ben Hei Hei, Pirke Avot (Sayings of the Fathers)
     5:27

If it were possible to simplify life to the utmost, how little one really wants! And is it a blessing or a disadvantage to be so made that one *must* take keen interest in many matters; that, seeing something that one's hand may do, one cannot resist doing or attempting it, even though time be already overcrowded, and strength much reduced, and sight steadily failing? Are the people happier who are content to drift comfortably down the stream of

life, to take things easily, not to *want* to take pains
or give themselves trouble about what is not exactly
necessary? I know not which, as worldly wisdom, is
the wiser; I only know that to my own mind and
conscience pure idleness seems to me akin to folly,
or even worse, and that in some form or other I
must obey the Divine command: 'Work while ye
have the light.'

ɔ *Gertrude Jekyll*, Home and Garden, *1900*

Help us to be always hopeful
Gardeners of the spirit
Who know that without darkness
Nothing comes to birth
As without light
Nothing flowers.

ɔ *May Sarton*, 'The Invocation to Kali', Selected
Poems of May Sarton, *1978*

Acknowledgements

Every effort has been made to trace and contact copyright holders and secure permission prior to printing. Hodder & Stoughton will be pleased to rectify any inadvertent errors or omissions in the next edition of this book.

Laurence Binyon, 'The Burning of the Leaves', from *The Burning of The Leaves and Other Poems*, MacMillan, 1944. Reprinted by permission of The Society of Authors as the Literary Representative of the Estate of Laurence Binyon.

Gerald Bullett, 'In the Garden at Night', from *Collected Poems*, Dent, 1936. Reprinted by

Michael Hamburger, 'Weeding', from *Collected Poems*, Carcanet Press, 1985. Reprinted by permission of the Michael Hamburger Estate and the publisher.

Susan Hill and Rory Stuart, extracts from *Reflections from a Garden*, Pavilion, 1995.

Jane Kenyon, 'Peonies at Dusk', from *Otherwise: New and Selected Poems*, Graywolf Press, © 1996 by the Estate of Jane Kenyon. Reprinted by permission of the Graywolf Press, Saint Paul, Minnesota.

Philip Larkin, 'Cut Grass', from *High Windows*, 1974. Reproduced by permission of Faber & Faber.

Anne Ridler, 'Winter Poem', from *The Collected Poems*, Carcanet Press, 1994.

Theodore Roethke, 'Long Live the Weeds', from *Collected Poems*, copyright © 1968. Reproduced by permission of Faber & Faber.